Dracula is a Racist

A Totally Factual Guide to Vampires

Matt Melvin

Illustrations by
D. J. Coffman and Matt Melvin

REBEL BASE BOOKS
Citadel Press
Kensington Publishing Corp.
www.kensingtonbooks.com

REBEL BASE BOOKS are published by

Kensington Publishing Corp.
119 West 40th Street
New York, NY 10018

Princess of the Night poster (p. 166) courtesy of Caballero Video.
Vampirella artwork (p. 180) by Joe Jusko, courtesy of Harris Publications.

All Kensington titles, imprints, and distributed lines are available at special quantity discounts for bulk purchases for sales promotions, premiums, fund-raising, educational, or institutional use. Special book excerpts or customized printings can also be created to fit specific needs. For details, write or phone the office of the Kensington special sales manager: Kensington Publishing Corp., 119 West 40th Street, New York, NY 10018, attn: Special Sales Department; phone 1-800-221-2647.

First printing: April 2010

10 9 8 7 6 5 4 3 2 1

Printed in the United States of America

Library of Congress Control Number: 2009937073

ISBN-13: 978-0-8065-3137-3
ISBN-10: 0-8065-3137-1

A Brief Introduction

Returning from the grave. Supernatural powers. Belief in the paranormal. With such inconceivable ideas, it's irrational to think a figure such as Jesus Christ could actually exist. But he does. Such is the predicament for vampires. Like the belief in Jesus, the belief in vampires has been in a steady decline for the past couple of centuries. This can be largely attributed to Hollywood spreading its perception of the fictional vampire: refined English gentlemen who wear long, fancy capes and frilly, ruffled shirts or devil worshippers who wear eyeliner and listen to nothing but Swedish death metal.

The latter group has actually spawned a subculture of angsty teenagers with a penchant for black clothing. These kids have very few friends and claim to refuse to interact with other people because they despise humans, regardless of the fact that they hang out in groups at the mall all day judging people. They even refer to themselves as vampyres—spelled with a *y*. Vampyres aren't real vampires, though; just like womyn aren't real lesbians.

As much as they may argue against it, this way of life is really nothing more than a fashion trend. In fact, to continue the charade, some go as far as to have dental work to have caps attached to their teeth so it looks like they have actual vampire fangs. Like, oh my God, these guys are seriously such total posers.

With these laughable misconceptions becoming part of our daily lives, it's no wonder that the belief in real vampires has been dwindling. Dracula, for example, is easily the most well-known vampire of all time, but most people are completely unaware that he actually exists, much less that he's a seething racist.

The truth about vampires has been replaced with fantasized visions of high-budget theatrics and special effects. Sure, huge explosions may look cool, but real vampires don't burst into a bright cloud of ash and smoke when stabbed in the heart with a stake. Real vampires don't all have aristocratic, foreign accents. Real vampires hate My Chemical Romance. And believe me, vampires definitely are real.

So what is a vampire? In simple terms, a vampire is a type of revenant, a being believed to have returned from the grave. Like a zombie except way more cool, a fact that will be pointed out several times throughout this book. The term comes from the French and Latin *revenir*, meaning "to return" or "to be bitten by a Goth asshole" (figure 1). These specific revenants have various qualities that set them apart from the others. Vampires are seductive, intelligent, artfully sly; do not act on pure impulse; and don't smell like a pile of decomposing flesh, making them the most dangerous and frightening of all the undead.

Figure 1. "Dick!"

Part of the fear and fascination with these beings comes from the mystery behind them. Just the thought of the un-dead brings up several questions on life and death, such as:

- What happens to people when they die?
- Does God exist?
- Is there such a place as Heaven or Hell?
- Does masturbating on an airplane qualify you for the mile-high club?
- Who let the dogs out?

None of these questions can be answered with any sort of certainty, especially when combined with the conflicting views from various religions, faiths, and Baha Men from around the world. We are, however, able to gather information relating to vampirism in order to better inform ourselves on the subject.

Everything contained in these pages is undisputed fact, culled from centuries of research, scientific experimentation, firsthand accounts, documentary evidence, and a wide collection of fictional works on the subject. While there is no such thing as a certified vampire historian or scientist (the title simply just does not exist), your author, who sometimes slips into the third person, is as close to being one as possible.[1]

Whether you want to learn how to better protect yourself from a vampire attack, are interested in training to hunt vampires, actually want to become a vampire yourself, or have re-

---

1. He read the vampire Wikipedia entry. Twice!

Fuck You

Jeff Rector, zombies

Contents

A Brief Introduction   xi

SECTION 1: HISTORY

1. Famous Vampires   3
2. Transylvania   25
3. Around the World   34
4. Migration   43
5. Etymology   47

SECTION 2: FACT VS. FICTION

6. Powers   53
7. Misconceptions   67
8. Vampiric Behavior   81

SECTION 3: KILL OR BE KILLED

9. Defending Yourself   93
10. To Kill a Vampire   101
11. The Thrill of the Hunt   108

Section 4: Living with Vampirism

12. Faking It   131
13. Becoming One   142
14. Life of a Vampire   149
15. Let's All Go to the Movies   157
16. Other Media   171

A Brief Conclusion   187

Thank You

My family, Rob DenBleyker, Dave McElfatrick, Kris Wilson, Steve Parker, Joe Peacock, Patrick Mulligan, Byrd Leavell, Richard Ember, D. J. Coffman

cently been turned into one, the information contained here is vital.

Before any of that, though, we must gain a greater understanding of what it means to be a vampire. We'll begin by looking at the more famous vampires along with a brief history of the birthplace of the modern vampire myth, Transylvania, and other various references to vampiric behavior from around the world. We'll continue with a look at the attributes that make vampires what they are, along with many of the common misconceptions perpetuated throughout popular culture. For further reading, the final two chapters contain the most influential vampire movies, TV shows, comic books, and more—information a discussion on vampirism wouldn't be complete without.

All of this information will give you the necessary tools and knowledge to better prepare yourself, whatever your prerogative. Without the proper information, the world of vampires can only be that much more dangerous.

While there is much to learn about these seductive bloodsuckers, if you take anything from this book, let it be the knowledge that vampires are totally way cooler than zombies.

Section 1

History

1. Famous Vampires

Vampirism wouldn't be as prevalent a topic as it is today if it weren't for the popularization of a few specific vampires. These individuals have become the celebrities of the vampire world. Rather than tabloid articles and sex tapes though, stories and songs have been written, movies have been filmed, and crappy Halloween costumes have been mass-produced in Taiwan.

To gain a better understanding of the world of vampires, we must look at their entire history. Before we dive into the historical account of the vampire, though, let's take a look at those specific vampires who helped shape the image we commonly associate with them today. And what better vampire to start with than the most famous vampire of them all, Dracula.

Dracula

Without a doubt, Dracula is the most well-known vampire in history. First publicly mentioned by name in the biography written by Bram Stoker, *Dracula,* many believe him to be the first vampire to ever exist. While this may or may not be true, Dracula does seem to be the oldest known vampire still alive today, even if his perfect skin says otherwise. I wonder what kind of moisturizer he uses.

Dracula (real name Vlad Tepes, aka Vlad III) was born in 1431 in Wallachia, where his father, Vlad II, would later rule as Prince. That same year, before two nearly consecutive terms, Vlad II was given the title *Dracul,* meaning "dragon," and inducted into the Order of the Dragon, an elite Chivalric order of Europe. This esteemed honor was bestowed upon him for leading the Wallachian army and valiantly defending the land from the God-King Xerxes and his one million soldiers.

Dracula, the name that Vlad III adopted for himself, means "son of Dracul." In addition to continuing the name, Vlad III followed closely in his father's footsteps and ruled Wallachia himself in the late 1400s. During his rule, he was given the incredibly powerful moniker "Vlad the Impaler," for his unique way of dealing with his enemies: by impaling them on large stakes in the ground.

This method of dealing with his opponents wasn't limited to just his enemies, either. He was known to impale anyone who opposed him: traitors, repeat criminals, even his kids when they talked back to him (figure 2).

The "Impaler" name would later become ironic, given one of the popular means of dispatching vampires.

At the age of forty-six, after spending several years in prison, Vlad III was sentenced to death by beheading.

Figure 2. "This'll hurt you a lot more than it hurts me."

Little Known Fact

A human head remains conscious for approximately fifteen to twenty seconds after being severed.

Also Little Known Fact

The sexual term "giving head" comes from the act of the executioner giving the severed head to the person in charge of overseeing the execution, who would then proceed to skullfuck it.

Soon after his death, Vlad III returned from the grave with a nasty taste in his mouth as the Dracula we all know today.

Once he became a vampire, Dracula also developed a strong racial hatred (as the title of this book might suggest). In fact, he was a prominent proponent of the spread of racism, single-handedly bringing about the creation of the Ku Klux Klan. Although he wasn't a founding member or anything, the practices this group is now widely known for were all inspired by Dracula.

After witnessing Dracula destroying crucifixes, Klan members began doing the same by lighting huge crosses on fire. When they found out Dracula was an "undead spirit" they all took white sheets and started dressing up like ghosts. After Dracula slept with their cousins, so did they.

Nowadays, Dracula is still very much a racist, but acts as one in much subtler ways. Being animated and ostentatious is exactly what *they* do.

Nosferatu

Nosferatu! That name alone can chill the blood!
—*Johann Cavallius, Bremen historian*

Nosferatu, the title commonly given to the vampire known as Count Orlok, is actually just a synonym for "vampire" that's attributed to him rather than an actual name. The term is believed to have likely been derived from the Greek *nosophoros,* meaning "plague-carrier" or "sex symbol" (figure 3).

As a child, Orlok was never part of the popular crowd, mostly due to his stunningly unattractive features. From the day he was regretfully discarded from his mother's womb, Orlok suffered from a peculiar form of male-pattern baldness that affects infants and continues into

Figure 3. Count Orlok displaying some of that vampire supersexuality.

adulthood. Growing up bald is hard enough, but Orlok also suffered from maximus leprechauriclytis, also known as "big-ass elf ears." Normally, sufferers of the disease grow their hair long and let it drape over their ears. Or they just pretend to be really into *The Lord of the Rings*. Orlok, however, couldn't grow hair and *Lord of the Rings* didn't even exist at the time.

Orlok was also incredibly tall as a kid. He hit puberty at a very young age, and his bones grew so quickly that it caused issues with his posture. It also caused him to develop some weird, gangly fingers that totally creep me the hell out. With all of this combined, Orlok grew up as a pretty ugly kid. A childhood picture of him was even used by tabloid magazines, which dubbed him the "Bat Boy." Suffice it to say, Orlok's

appearance caused him to have a difficult time with the ladies when he was growing up.

That nervous stutter probably didn't help, either.

Being ostracized by women his entire life, Orlok grew up to be quite the misogynist. When coupled with his vampiric blood-lust, that misogyny turned into a deadly resentment of women. He became a psychological killer who targeted countless numbers of women and enacted his revenge upon them.

As Sigmund Freud would say, "Dude probably boned his mom, too."

Orlok detested the women he attacked so much that he never let any of his victims become vampires like him, instead choosing to kill them all before they turned (figure 4). Luckily for him, law enforcement during this period of time was nothing like the *CSI* crime wizards we have today, able to pinpoint their suspect based on the single semen sample that every dumb killer somehow always leaves at the crime scene. Orlok's victims were instead written off as casualties of the various plagues ravaging the area, leaving no suspicion of possible attacks. Because of this, Orlok was able to feed without any worry of being found.

Everything changed when Orlok became infatuated with a woman named Ellen Hutter. For some reason, Orlok saw something in Ellen that made him view her differently, admiring her from afar for quite some time. Could it be that

Figure 4. Count Orlok totally mackin' on some breezy.

Orlok, a man hell-bent on homicidal, blood-fueled misogyny, was capable of . . . love?

At first, Ellen thought Orlok was just a harmless rapist but eventually realized he was a vampire. She took it upon herself to rid the land of this monster, luring him into her bedroom just before daybreak in hopes of tricking him into staying in the sunlight. This act cost Ellen her life, but it worked. Orlok was so pussy whipped he didn't realize what was happening until it was too late. Trapped in Ellen's room with nowhere to hide, he was consumed by sunlight and burst into a pillar of smoke.

Count Chocula

Unlike most vampires, Count Chocula was friendly and nonviolent. His vampirism was the result of being attacked and turned against his will. He despised being a vampire and loathed being associated with blood-sucking murderers. As a vampire, he vowed he would never bring the same pain upon any human being.

This proved difficult, however, as the lust for blood is impossible to overcome by pure force of will. Like a fat dude with cake, Chocula felt powerless over his cravings. He began dealing with this by feeding on rats, stray cats and dogs, the homeless, and other animals nobody would care about if they were killed. Still, Chocula was unsatisfied with the life he had been forced into. He had to do something to change it.

Before becoming a vampire, Chocula was a brilliant research

chemist and scientist. He had no experience with vampires or bloodwork in the past, but his relative lack of knowledge in the field wasn't going to stop him from spending every waking moment trying to find a cure to somehow reverse the effects of his newfound vampirism.

While testing for a possibility to negate the cravings altogether, he had his first major breakthrough. Due to an accident during one of his experiments, he was somehow able to convert his lust for blood into a craving for chocolate breakfast cereals. This was a huge milestone but caused a slight problem: no cereal was ever good enough.

Cocoa Pebbles was all right, Cookie Crisp was just a joke, and, sure, Cocoa Puffs turned his milk brown with chocolaty goodness, but it was still missing something. Unsatisfied with the available options, Chocula took it upon himself to create the best chocolate breakfast cereal in existence.

This audacious endeavor had piqued the interest of Lieutenant Mills, a breakfast cereal connoisseur and businessman who would later rise to the rank of General. Mills recruited Chocula for a position in cereal research and development. With Mills's backing, the count spent years testing and experimenting with new combinations of cereal until he eventually found the missing piece of the puzzle he'd been searching for: marshmallows.

A popular Irish cereal at the time was filled to the brim with marshmallows—rainbows, blue moons, and a multitude of various other colors and shapes. Chocula noticed this and experimented with a combination of chocolate-flavored marshmallows and frosted cereal, eventually creating the best cereal ever to be produced (figure 5).

Figure 5. Cereal + Chocolate + Marshmallows = YAAAAY.

Mills was so pleased with the results that not only did he name the cereal after the count, but he made him the mascot for it as well. Chocula never intended on becoming a mascot when he first set out, but he fit the bill amazingly well. He soon became one of the most popular mascots of all time, way better than an enthusiastic furry in a tiger costume.[2]

Chocula never let this newfound success go to his head. He remained humble and kept close relations with his longtime friends. He even used his connections to get some of them, such as Franken Berry and Yummy Mummy, their very own cereals.

Bluebeard

As we will later learn, particularly violent or cruel sinners were apt to return from the grave as vampires. Bluebeard was definitely no exception.

2. They're grrrrrrross!

This dude was fucked up. Real name Gilles de Rais, Bluebeard was the alias given to him after he was convicted of infanticide—the torture, rape, and murder of children.

With a name like Bluebeard, one would assume him to be a pirate, but in fact he was nothing more than a European nobleman. Born in France in 1404, Gilles lost his father when he was only nine years old. After his mother died two years later, he and his brother were sent to live with his grandfather, a grouchy old man and total dick. His grandfather, in an effort to rid himself of the nuisance of taking care of "these ungrateful little shits," tried to pawn Gilles off by arranging for him to marry a prominent girl. His first attempt was the heiress Jeanne de Paynol, but she was mysteriously killed before the wedding. The second was Béatrice de Rohan, who was also mysteriously killed. The third time, with Catherine de Thouars, was a success, but only because Gilles's grandfather kidnapped her before anything could happen to her.[3]

Years later after his grandfather passed away, Gilles's sick perversion began.

A boy would be lured into his castle under false pretenses. Once inside, the boy would be tied up and hung upside down from the ceiling by rope or chains. Just before losing consciousness, the boy would be taken down and reassured that no harm would come to him. Gilles would then rape him (see figure 6, next page).

---

3. Take note, obsessive psychopaths. Sometimes you *do* have to take things into your own hands to ensure nothing gets in the way of your love!

It only got worse from there. The ensuing actions Gilles took part in have been deemed too foul to be reiterated in these pages. Suffice it to say, the actions perpetrated by this man make those of the most heinous serial killers and pedophiles look like mere child's play. In addition to this, he was also known to smoke drugs and litter!

Figure 6. "Tricked you!"

Gilles's obsession with the forbidden led him to become interested in black magic. An evil magician suggested he sell his soul to the devil to further his "journey." But Gilles was a devout Catholic and his morals wouldn't allow him to do such a thing. Instead, he raped and murdered some more little boys.

Gilles's actions were soon discovered when the bodies of dozens of these boys were uncovered. With incriminating testimony from his servants, he was convicted and condemned to death. Because his actions were so heinous, the court sentenced him to be strangled and stabbed to death by the families of the children he had killed. Brutal.

Don't forget, all of this happened before he ever became a vampire. These were the actions of a normal human being. Well, not mentally normal, but physiologically normal.

Amusingly enough, when he actually did become a vampire, he completely stopped pursuing his old, sadistic ways.

As a human, he was obsessed with the sinful aspect, the wickedness, of what he was doing. As a vampire, however, that sadism really paled in comparison to what all vampires did on a frequent basis. Sure, he was a little more violent than most when he eventually sought his revenge on the servants who had testified against him and the families who had condemned him to death, but mutilation and rape just seemed so passé.

The worst part of it all, though? His beard wasn't even blue. What a fraud.

Lestat de Lioncourt

Lestat, the vampire famously portrayed by Tom Cruise in *Interview with the Vampire* and Stuart Townsend in *Queen of the Damned*, is known to be extremely vain, bold, arrogant, and reluctant to follow orders. Inside the vampire realm, he was chastised for this by his elders, often referring to him as "the Brat Prince," a title he is quite fond of. However, outside of the vampire world, he's much better known for his interest and aspirations in U.S. politics, which he pursued under his other name, Richard Nixon.

After serving in the navy during WWII, he was elected to Congress to be California's twelfth district representative and later its senator. After unsuccessful political runs in 1960 and 1962, Lestat was elected to the presidency in 1968, becoming the thirty-seventh president of the United States.

"Tricky Lestat," as he was sometimes referred to, had a strong first term and was reelected for a second. Things went south soon after, the turning point being the Watergate scandal. Five burglars were caught breaking into the Democratic Party headquarters at the Watergate Hotel on June 17, 1972, bringing to light several instances of phone tapping of journalists and administration officials, an assassination request of newspaper columnist Jack Anderson, and the cover-up of an investigation of the president's possible vampirism (figure 7).

Two reporters from the *Washington Post*, Bob Woodward and Carl Bernstein, began to pursue the truth behind the scandal. "Deep Throat," the pseudonym given to Deputy Director of the FBI Linda Lovelace (who moonlighted as an adult film

Figure 7. "I am not a crook. Or a vampire."

actress), acted as a secret informant for Woodward and Bernstein, supplying them with inside information regarding the scandal, internal Watergate documents, and copious amounts of oral sex.

With impeachment looming, Nixon resigned from office, never to return to politics again. He now performs in the rock band The Vampire Lestat.

Things Richard Nixon Is Also Not Besides a Crook

- A serial killer
- A tax evasionist
- A petty thief
- An arsonist
- An Old West bank robber
- A cat burglar
- A drug dealer
- A timely subject matter

Count von Count

Count von Count—or the Count, as he's more commonly referred to—currently lives on *Sesame Street*. With a name like Count von Count, it's no coincidence that he really enjoys counting. To say he just enjoys it, though, is a significant understatement. Simply counting to three causes him to erupt in maniacal, boisterous laughter.

This seemingly innocent fondness of counting is actually a side effect of a severe case of obsessive compulsive disorder. OCD usually causes sufferers to perform various actions a specific number of times to prevent some alleged event or situation from occurring, but the Count suffers from a very specific type of OCD known as arithmomania. Sufferers of arithmomania feel compelled to obsessively and meticulously count their actions or objects in their surroundings. The castle the count lives in, for example, is home to a large number of bats that the count often feels subconsciously obligated to count.

Aside from just being weird, this disorder also causes the Count an immense amount of trouble when it comes to hunting for fresh blood. He often finds himself distracted by his surroundings, causing him to stop the pursuit of his would be victims to count various objects. For instance, during his pursuit of the Cookie Monster, the count stumbled upon the Cookie Monster's vast supply of cookies. And when sneaking up on Oscar the Grouch, the count was bombarded with the immense amount of fleas crawling around on his furry body.

The Count's arithmomania is so severe that if he hasn't counted anything after a certain amount of time, he'll feel the need to do so even if there is nothing around to count. "When I'm alone, I count myself. One count!" You sad, sad man. Luckily for the count, he has quite a way with women, so loneliness isn't much of a problem.

The Count used to share his castle with his former girlfriend, Countess von Backwards. They shared a common "interest"

in counting. Von Backwards had a sort of reverse arithmomania, in that she felt the need to count just as the Count
did but done backwards. In order to do this, though, she would
have to know the total of what she was counting beforehand.
So she already knew the number but still felt compelled to
count—a sign of an even more severe case of arithmomania
than the Count's.

Von Backwards and the Count's relationship began to sour
over the years, the turning point coming from the introduction of Countess Dahling von Dahling. Von Dahling looked
remarkably similar to von Backwards: same general hairstyle,

physique, and cute little puppet mouth. The Count was immediately intrigued.

Being the only count on all of Sesame Street, it wasn't hard to attract both countesses. Convincing both to participate in a threesome proved to be much more difficult.[4] The threesome eventually happened, but it solidified von Backwards's worries that the relationship was over, resulting in her leaving the Count soon after. The Count is currently dating von Dahling, who has since moved into his castle with him.

Vampires > Zombies: The Fabulous Life

There are so many famous vampires! They're like the rock stars of the monster world. Without even reading this book, I bet you could ask anybody and that person would be able to tell you at least one of their names. Are there any famous zombies, though? Nope. Losers.

Grandpa and Lily Munster

Lily Munster and her father, aptly named Grandpa, are part of the classic American sitcom family, *The Munsters,* which includes Lily's husband, Herman; son, Eddie; and niece, Marilyn. Although the family considered themselves

4. "C'mon, baby, it'll be fun. The three of us, you know, 1, 2, 3, AH AH AH!!"

to be a typical middle-class family, they definitely stood out in their community. A creepy castlelike mansion and Gothic-styled car in a suburban neighborhood really stand out. Not to mention their fire breathing T-rex they kept as a pet under the staircase. Marilyn, the only normal one in the family, was the only one who found it easy to fit in. It was difficult for everyone else, though, since they were all monsters of some sort.

This brings up an interesting point: Lily, a vampire, and Herman, a Frankenstein monster, had a son, Eddie, who was a werewolf. How does that work? Is this the first subtle reference of adultery (possibly even bestiality) to make its way onto broadcast television?

The family, who immigrated to the United States in search of a better life, has warmed our hearts with their goofy antics and charming attempts to integrate into society. Regardless of two of them being blood-sucking vampires, I think we can all agree they were much nicer than those snobby jerks in *The Addams Family*.

Count Duckula

First appearing to a wide audience in the British animated TV show *DangerMouse*, Count Duckula is the first and only vampire duck in existence and one of DangerMouse's many sworn enemies.

DangerMouse, who is indeed a mouse, is the greatest secret agent in the world. He is best known for his fashionable eyepatch, which he actually has no need to wear. He simply enjoys experiencing bad depth perception. DangerMouse is aided by his sidekick, Ernest Penfold, a cowardly and timid hamster who wears glasses and a blue business suit.

Like all of DangerMouse's enemies, Count Duckula held a severe resentment for the rodent superspy. Duckula's hatred was unique, though. For as long as he could remember, Duckula was absolutely obsessed with show business. He was desperate to have his own show. Being a supporting character on DangerMouse's show made him incredibly envious.

Much to his surprise, seven years after *DangerMouse* premiered, Count Duckula was given his very own show in the form of a spin-off series. The series featured a slew of characters, almost all of which were anthropomorphized birds. Like any good vampire, Duckula had his own Van Helsing antagonist character, Dr. Von Goosewing. Duckula was also accompanied by his butler, Igor, and his aptly named nanny, Nanny.

The show also featured a unique view into the nature of life and death. Duckula was killed several times but was constantly reincarnated through a blood ritual by his servants. Just the kind of wholesome content parents want in a kid's show.

During the ritual for the current incarnation of Duckula, his servants accidentally used ketchup instead of blood, which resulted in the count being a vegetarian. Besides Count Chocula, this makes him the only other vampire to not drink blood. It also gives him a much better chance at hooking up with that cute vegan chick who works at the coffee shop.

The Fresh Count of Bel-Air

Sir William the Fresh, a young vampire from West Philadelphia, born and raised, spent most of his days on the playground. William enjoyed spending most of his time with his friends, or as they liked to say, "chillin' out," "maxin'," or "relaxin' all cool."

Aside from drinking human blood, William played a lot of basketball outside of his school. One day while "chillin' out" with his compatriots, William was accosted by a group of local vampire hunters. He was able to escape unharmed, but the news of this altercation quickly reached William's mother. Frightened, she immediately arranged for William to be sent to live with his aunt and uncle in Bel-Air.

William hailed for a cab and was quickly greeted by a peculiar sight. The taxi that awaited him was adorned with a custom license plate that said "FRESH" and had a pair of dice hanging from the rearview mirror. It was quite the rare sight. Upon entering the vehicle, William was met with quite a pungent odor. The odor wasn't garlic, but the stale stench of the taxi driver. It was so strong, however, that it might as well have been garlic. William very much wished to "smell [him] later."

The ride was unbearable, but the taxi eventually arrived at his destination. William exited the vehicle, excused his driver, and set his eyes upon his new kingdom. The drastic change of scenery had effectively "flipped-turned" William's life upside down. He gazed upon this new land: a pure, untapped source of new victims. From that day forth, William reigned atop a throne of human skulls as the Fresh Count of Bel-Air.

2. Transylvania

We are in Transylvania, and Transylvania is not England. Our ways are not your ways, and there shall be to you many strange things. Nay, from what you have told me of your experiences already, you know something of what strange things there may be.
—*Count Dracula* (Dracula, *1897)*

Even the less geographically inclined of us have some kind of knowledge of Transylvania. Known to many as the home of the most well-known vampire of them all, Dracula, Transylvania serves as a historical vampire provenance of sorts. But is this place even real? If so, where is it? Is it in a nice neighborhood? Would you recommend it as a family vacation spot? What kinds of time-share options are available?

There are actually several places that go by the name Transylvania, many of which can be found in the United States.

Transylvania, the North Carolina County

There's a small county in North Carolina called Transylvania. There's really nothing else about it worth mentioning.

Figure 8. A North Carolinian vampire doing what he does best:
discriminating against black people.

It's North Carolina after all. They do have a ton of Confeder-
ate flags (figure 8).

Transylvania, the Louisiana Community

In East Carroll Parish, Louisiana, there's a little community that goes by the name Transylvania. Being a parish, it's a

widely religious area and contains a large amount of churches, which is ironic for a place so closely related to vampirism. The community is home to the Transylvania General Store, which sells vampire- and bat-related merchandise to travelers passing through. This lively community also features a post office, a water tower, and an immense amount of dirt.

Transylvania, the University

Transylvania University is a liberal arts college located in Lexington, Kentucky. Once again, it also has ironically close ties with Christianity, relating to the Protestant congregation of the Christian Church (Disciples of Christ).

It's uncertain what leads religious people toward using a name already heavily associated with the occult. One reason could be the idea of reappropriation, taking a term that was used negatively and turning it back into something positive, much like feminists did with the word *bitch*[5] or homosexuals did with the word *fag*.[6]

The school itself is home to approximately 1,100 students, over half of which are members of a Greek organization. Many fraternities and sororities have chapters at "Transy"—as it's commonly referred to—including the illustrious Delta Sigma Phi (ΔΣΦ), Delta Delta Delta (ΔΔΔ), and the Jewish frat Phi Kappa Menorah (ΦΚΨ).

5. You go, girls!
6. You go, girls!

Transylvania, the Henderson Colony

For a short while, there was a colony that once existed in an area spanning between what is now Kentucky and Tennessee that went by the name Transylvania. In 1775, American pioneer and merchant Richard Henderson of North Carolina purchased the area from the Cherokee Indians during a meeting with their leader, Chief Attakullakulla (figure 9).

Henderson hired famous American trailblazer Daniel Boone to establish the Wilderness Trail, a principal route of travel that was used for more than fifty years by thousands of people. The trail stretched from Fort Chiswell in Virginia,

Figure 9. Yo, I'm Chief Attakullakulla / Don't mess with no Dracula / Sold all of Transylvania / Just to score some more crackulla / Jyeah!

through the Cumberland Gap and into central Kentucky, right through the Transylvania colony. During his trailblazing efforts, Boone came across the Kansas River. While attempting to ford the river, he lost three oxen, two spare wheels, 120 pounds of food, and Maggie died of dysentery.[7]

While not all of it is used for travel, most of the trail can still be seen today. A portion of the trail was among the first roads in the United States to be paved, the Cumberland Gap is now a national park, and portions of the Wilderness Trail can be visited at the Wilderness Road State Park in Virginia.

The colony, however, did not share the same lasting effect. In 1776, a mere one year after Henderson obtained the land, Virginia invalidated the purchase and the colony ceased to exist. Henderson went on record to proclaim, "Thanks, Virginia. Dicks."

Transylvania, the Space Galaxy

In the movie *The Rocky Horror Picture Show*, Tim Curry plays a transvestite[8] alien from the planet Transexual [*sic*]. Transylvania is the name of the galaxy that the planet can be found in. The other aliens, after shooting a few people with their  three-barrel laser gun, blast off into the sky in their mansion spaceship, presumably through a time warp of some sort.

7. Shouldn't have set your pace to grueling . . .
8. A little too convincingly.

Transylvania, the Romanian Province

Transylvania is also the name of a fictional region of Romania, which is referenced in a large amount of vampire-related literature. While this area doesn't actually exist, the stories and history behind it are so vast and rich with detail that we are able to visually construct the area with no problem (figure 10).

The geography of Transylvania is, for the most part, identical to that of the region of Romania it was set in: a heavily forested, typical European landscape. The name Transylvania is actually said to come from the Latin meaning of "beyond the forest."

Figure 10. A map of Romania with what the region of Transylvania would look like if it was real.

It's said that when a boy hit puberty, he would make the journey all the way from the heavily forested Skrotem and Testiqiuliu regions in the south to the northernmost part of the Transylvanian territory, the Forest Kin. This rite of passage into manhood, done alone and in the middle of the night, was known as the "nocturnal expedition."

A detailed coat of arms was even created for Transylvania (figure 11). The sun and moon, respectively, represent life and death (or, more appropriately, the undead that come out at night). The black bird between them is a turul, a mythological bird of Hungarian origin believed to protect the living from the undead. After realizing the belief in a fake bird won't help protect someone from a vampire attack, the red dividing band was added, representing the river of blood that flowed due to the Transylvanian people's lowered guards. The seven towers, based on a popular prophecy among the Transylvanians, represent the number

Figure 11. The Transylvanian coat of arms.

of days before you die after watching a crappy excuse for a black-and-white surrealist art film about a girl in a well, usually noted by receiving a creepy, whispered phone call soon afterward.[9]

One of the more well-known features of Transylvania,

9. "Seven daaaaayssss . . ."

had it actually existed, would be that of Bran Castle, which would have been more commonly known as "Dracula's Castle." Situated on the border between Transylvania and Wallachia, the castle would rest atop the edge of a steep cliff, and, when given the right angle, would look super creepy at night.

Today, the castle would serve as a national monument and landmark. Travelers from far and wide would come to visit the castle, which would be transformed into a museum. Guided tours would be available to take tourists through the interior of the castle, displaying classic Romanian architecture, art, and furniture. A small, open-air park would also exhibit traditional Romanian peasant structures from throughout the country. If it actually existed, of course.

Vampires > Zombies: Location, Location, Location

Transylvania sounds like a pretty awesome place. It's the veritable home of what we know as the modern vampire. It's got castles, coffins, creepy plants, and all sorts of crazy European stuff, not to mention a well-known history surrounding vampires. And what about zombies—where do they come from? Nowhere.

Transylvania, the Truth

Oddly enough, *The Rocky Horror Picture Show* was actually the closest to the truth. In the early sixteenth century, there was an abundance of transvestites living in Pennsylvania. For those who lived there, this was common, but it was quite a different sight for those not accustomed to the area.

One such passerby, a refined gentleman by the name of Herbert P. Wilcox, was traveling through the area on a trip with several members from the Refined Gentlemen's Club. Wilcox noticed this high concentration of trannies and commented to his traveling companions, "Pennsylvania? More like *Tran*sylvania! Am I right!?" They all shared a hearty laugh among each other.

One of those companions was none other than novelist Bram Stoker, who later used the name as the homeland of the main character in the previously mentioned biography, *Dracula*.

That's right, what most of us know as the birthplace of the most famous vampire in history is actually just a slang term coined by a man who enjoyed making fun of transvestites.

So if Transylvania isn't the actual origin of the vampire and is really just a myth, where do vampires come from then?

3. Around the World

The history behind the vampire stretches far and wide, reaching even the most remote places all around the world. Some occurrences are just misinterpretations and not true incidences of vampiric behavior, but upon scientifically researching each case, many have been found to be genuine.

One such misinterpretation came during the Irish Potato Famine from the mid 1840s to the early 1850s. Also known as "The Great Hunger" in Ireland itself, it was the result of a pathogenic water mold that destroyed potato crops throughout the entire country. The disease was the cause of the deaths of approximately 20 to 25 percent of the entire population. Maybe if you didn't use potatoes for everything you wouldn't have to worry about running out of them. . . .

In order to survive, many people were forced to drink the blood of farm animals. Some were believed to have become so accustomed to it that they began roaming the countryside looking for new victims. These, of course, were just your typical Galway residents and not real vampires. However, these memories are still so strong that they continue to haunt the

Irish today, causing the entire nation to deal with their regret through the consumption of copious amounts of Guinness and Bushmills.

The earliest real recorded reference to vampires comes from ancient Assyrian tablets, which reference creatures they called the ekimmu, thin and sickly undead who drank the blood of people who were nearing death. Because of these tablets, some believe Assyria to be the place of origin of vampires, but numerous other prominent references to vampires appear throughout the world.

Philippines

While not technically one of the undead, the aswang[10] of the Philippines were living people who would transform into birds and hide in the trees waiting for people who were too sick or weak to fight back so they could drink their blood. These people were usually female, which, really, is just typical. First they get us kicked out of the Garden of Eden and now this? And they still bitch about not getting equal pay? C'mon, ladies.

India

The act of becoming a vampire can happen in several different ways (more on this in chapter 13, "Becoming One"). The churel of India were said to have been women who died

10. Heh, ass wang.

during childbirth or while menstruating, which ties into their thirst for blood. These particular vampires were said to be incredibly ugly, with unnaturally long and thick, black tongues; thick, rough lips; wild, messy hair; sagging breasts; and backward feet. They were thought to be angry and bitter due to their unfortunate deaths, or maybe they were just angry at the way people described them.

Medieval Europe

The people of medieval Europe have what they refer to as the incubus, a male demon who would prey upon human women and drain their energy while having sex with them. Some sources indicate that an incubus could be identified by its unnaturally cold penis. That doesn't really help safeguard you against attacks, though, because if you're feeling one's penis it's already way too late.

And yes, the band Incubus did name itself after this. The idea of a monster capable of sucking so much instantly clicked with the band.

The incubus also has a female counterpart, the succubus, known for similarly draining its victims' energy during inter-course. While "succubus" is the most commonly used term, na-tive women also often referred to them by various other names, such as "whores," "scarlets" and "skeezy skank bitches."

Being attacked by one of these monsters obviously isn't something you'd wish upon yourself, but out of all the ways to go, being exhausted to death through intense lovemaking really doesn't seem all that bad. It sure as hell beats dying of the plague.

Australia

Aboriginal tribes throughout Australia have tales of what they call the yara-ma-yha-who. Described as a short red man with a big head and large mouth with no teeth, this monster was said to enjoy fig trees and taking naps after attacking its victims. Investigations have shown, however, that these "beasts" were nothing more than agitated elderly men with sunburns.

Judaism

The Jewish people have stories of what they call the mohel, a man who would take newborn, male babies and very meticulously cut the foreskin off their penises and suck their

blood from it, a form of ritual circumcision commonly referred to as a bris.

It goes without saying, but ceremonial penile mutilation is best to avoid. Luckily, mohels have several distinct habits and mannerisms that are easy to recognize, making it relatively simple to spot and avoid them altogether.

For starters, mohels only ever seem to feed on male babies, never female. This could be because only male babies have the necessary anatomy to perform circumcisions on, or it could be because of deep psychological fears of women, most likely due to all the verbal abuse sustained from their mothers when they were children. Regardless, if you spot what looks like a shy, timid man becoming awkward and flustered around women, there's a very high chance that person is actually a vampire.

Mohels are also known for their particular habits of hunting for fresh blood in or around banks, Asian restaurants, and massage parlors. Due to the high frequency of sightings in these areas, it's best to try to avoid them at all costs unless it is absolutely necessary.

Armenia

Dakhanavar, also known as Dashnavar, is a specific vampire who lived in the Armenian mountains and attacked travelers. What makes this vampire worth mentioning is his unique form of feeding. At night, he would sneak up on travelers while they slept and suck their blood from their feet.

However, it's a widely known fact that all Armenians have weird-ass foot fetishes, so this really doesn't come as much of a surprise.

China

The jianshi, more commonly known as the Chinese hopping vampires, were believed to have returned from the grave due to improper burials. They hopped, rather than walked, as a result of a combination of midstage rigor mortis and China's immense love for Super Mario Bros. Rather than feeding on human blood, they sucked out "life force." And gold coins.

Germany

The doppelsauger is one of many types of European vampires who all share an obsession with their victims' breasts. In this case, the doppelsauger, which literally translates to "double sucker," will consume the breasts of its victim after feeding. This breast fixation is found only in Europe, along with unisex bathrooms and the metric system. Weirdos.

Baby Mamas

Found primarily in the United States, Baby Mamas are women who purposely get pregnant with a man they aren't married to in an attempt to trick them into sticking around or, at the very least, paying child support so they can monetarily suck them dry.

Facebook

Found solely on the Internet,[11] Facebook vampires pose no actual threat beyond minor annoyance. And even then, they're only mildly more annoying than being poked, but not quite as annoying as being SuperPoked. On the plus side, they are currently waging an e-war against the Facebook zombies and werewolves.

Hollywood

Most stories of vampires end as just stories. Hard evidence can be almost impossible to come by. Vampires are notorious for duping those around them and concealing their true nature, even those in the movie industry. Many of these "Hollywood vampires" are eventually found out, but not before creating dozens of movies, resulting in some of the most well-documented accounts of vampirism to date.

Jim Belushi, for example, doesn't show the usual physical characteristics of a vampire, but be assured that he could suck the life out of anything. For reference, you can refer to his roles in *According to Jim*; *Taking Care of Business*; *K-9*; *K-911*; *K-9: P.I.*; *Underdog*; *Joe Somebody*; *Jingle all the Way*; *Race the Sun*; *Abraxas, Guardian of the Universe*; *Curly Sue*; *Mr. Destiny*; *Red Heat*;

---

11. Also known as "teh intarweb."

Figure 12. Douche.

and of course *Tugger: The Jeep 4x4 Who Wanted to Fly.* The list goes on.

It should be pointed out that we're talking about Jim Belushi and not his late brother, John. Besides being brothers, they share very little in common. One is a human; the other isn't. One is an incredibly talented performer; the other isn't. One is a comedy icon; the other was awarded the title "Funniest Living Belushi." By default.

In fact, Jim bears more of a resemblance to co-vampire "actor" Steven Seagal than to John. It's uncanny, really. Same receding hairline, same amount of acting skill, same unwelcomed musical aspirations, same I'm-always-cringing-because-I-know-how-much-of-a-douche-bag-I-am face (figure 12). Really, the whole shebang.

4. Migration

Vampires have been known throughout the world for centuries, but there seems to be a growing number of them in the United States. How did this higher-than-normal concentration come to be exactly? Migration.

Vampires are a nomadic species by nature. This frequent need for a change of scenery is due to three specific details of vampire life: living in the same place for too long can get incredibly mundane, the variety of available prey can be somewhat limited, and vampire hunters become more likely to track them down. Basic survival instincts, for any predator, boil down to these same basic principles of territory expansion, hunting, and self-preservation. As immortals, however, these become that much more apparent.

Even humans, with their finite life spans, can't stand to live in the same place for too long. After a while, we all just want a change of scenery. Immortals feel this compulsive need for relocation even more so. It's like how old people are always traveling. After living in the same place for so many years, they just need to get out. Mahjong and bridge are fun for only so long, after all. After a while, you just feel the need to go on a drunken bender around Europe for a month.

Prey also becomes an issue. Running out of available prey isn't a problem, but getting tired of feeding on the same prey every time is. Vampires are creatures of discerning taste. They desperately need to avoid the mundane. It's like eating at a really good burger joint: it's great to begin with, but after a while you just don't want burgers anymore. After feeding on nothing but Italians, vampires just feel like some Chinese.

The primary cause for this continual relocation, however, is the threat that vampire hunters pose. Slayers are a vampire's biggest fear. It's only logical to keep a safe distance if a hunter is getting too close.

Slayers' influence on the vampire population actually brings up some interesting insights on natural selection. Assorted groups of vampires around the globe developed varying ways of dealing with the threat of slayers. The groups who survived were the ones able to adapt new techniques, a perfect example of real independent development via natural selection.

As Charles Darwin once said, "Eventually, only those with the capability to adapt will be able to survive. The endangered species list, for example, is basically just a directory of loser animals. Documentation of 'survival of the fittest' in action."

Migration to Immigration

The nomadic nature of vampires has actually caused immigration issues along the border between the United States and Mexico. The government is adamant about calling these border-hopping vampires "illegal aliens," but it should be noted that they are in no way aliens of any kind.

The authorities fear these vampires want to enter the United States to drink the blood of innocent Americans and, even worse, obtain green cards. This has sparked quite an intense immigration debate, with supporters of both sides making their case. Bias aside, allowing immigration has several pros and cons:

PROS:

- Free labor market
- Cultural diversity
- Clean dishes
- Readily available, high-quality landscaping

CONS:

- Welfare abuse
- Labor competition
- National security
- Health problems
- Fruit picked too efficiently

Several unplanned side effects have already affected the nation as well, some of which have been positive, some negative. On the positive side, for example, is the introduction of hot sauce, which Mexican vampires use on everything. Many meals and dishes have been livened up by this simple ingredient. It also helped with the introduction of various authentic Mexican restaurants, like Taco Bell, throughout the nation.

On the negative side, however, we've noticed the introduction of a peculiar new breed of mice. These fast-running rodents all seem to wear yellow, oversized sombreros and red ascots. According to multiple sources, these mice "know everybody's sister," and are considered a sexual threat to any female they encounter.

5. Etymology

Does the word "duh" mean anything to you?
—*Buffy* (Buffy the Vampire Slayer, *1992)*

The term "vampire" has a history all its own. The *Oxford English Dictionary* dates the first appearance of the word in the English language from 1734 in Europe. The term was derived from the Czechoslovakian "vampire," which is itself a derivation from the Greek vocabulary.

Like the Greeks, the Czechs have an immense admiration for sports and physical competitions. The single most popular sport among the Czechs—one that was, again, taken from the Greeks—is baseball. The Czechs copied every detail of the game from their Greek brothers, down to the exact terms being used (figure 13, p. 48).

The language barrier between the two cultures caused several of these terms to be misinterpreted. In old Greek lettering, letters were written using only straight lines, causing their *U*s to look like *V*s. So "Umpire," the position of the official

Figure 13. Baseball: the great Czechoslovakian pastime.

in charge of overseeing the game, became "Vmpire" when incorrectly translated (figure 14, opposite).

This error went unnoticed, primarily due to the Czechs' already overwhelming use of consonants. When translated to English, an extra vowel was added to make it pronounceable, becoming "vampire."

At first, the term wasn't actually used to describe what we now know as vampires at all.

When stories of real vampires began spreading around the

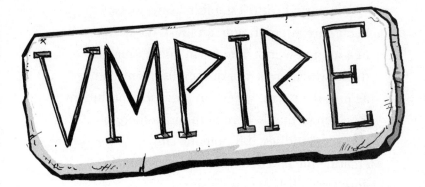

Figure 14. That's totally a *U*.

world, the sports announcer Marv Albert equated the actions of these monsters with notably bad calls various umpires made during games: "Oh, what a call! This vampire is literally sucking the blood from these Padres. BOOM-SHAKALAKA!" Like many of his catchphrases, this caught on, quickly becoming part of everyday vernacular.

The term officially became part of the English language when it was added to various prominent English dictionaries in the mid to late 1700s. Mrs. Merriam Webster herself discussed the inclusion of this word in an interview:

> When first deciding on the official word, we were quite torn. The popular term being used, you see, was a lingual mishap. We determined it was in our best interest to produce an original word in place of it.

> We started with "establish," since these
> beings are attempting to establish themselves
> in a human world. The norm doesn't include
> them, which gives us a disestablishment. Being
> against the norm, we get an antidisestablishment.
> The beings that believe in this idea therefore
> become antidisestablishmentarians,
> creating the all-encompassing ideal of
> antidisestablishmentarianism.
>
> We realized the word was ginormous so we
> just said screw it and used "vampire."

After the term was officially introduced into the English lexicon, slang terms immediately began arising. For example, vampire also became a term used to describe people who performed oral sex on women during their periods.

Section 2

Fact vs. Fiction

6. Powers

Let's just be blunt here: superpowers are freaking awesome. Flying, seeing through walls, invisibility—they're all so cool! Comic book nerds' obsessive interest in them is even attractive to beautiful women![12] And vampires? They got the pick of the litter, some of the coolest powers available.

The following is an in-depth look at those powers. You may notice that several of the powers commonly associated with vampires are not included. This is, once again, because the common archetype of the vampire is partially disconnected from the truth. Several of the powers we currently associate with vampires are really nothing more than myth and hearsay. These falsely attributed powers will be addressed in the next chapter, "Misconceptions."

However, in place of these incorrectly recognized powers are several other abilities not commonly known to the general public, "unknown" abilities that either are rarely mentioned or have just been completely forgotten over time. All these

12. Stan Lee is swimming in poontang.

powers combined make vampires one of the most powerful (if not the most powerful) monsters alive.

Immortality

Unending life is one of the most powerful abilities in existence. Never growing old and having (literally) all the time in the world to pursue your desires makes immortality easily the most sought-after power of them all. Immortals are able to be killed, but not by any natural means. Highlanders, for example, can be killed only by decapitation or an overwhelming amount of reruns on network television.[13]

As far as vampires go, the rules to immortality are fairly simple: you don't age and you need to feed only on blood. The age you remain is based on when you were turned. So if you were bitten, you remain the same age as when you were bitten. If you've returned from the grave, you remain the same age as when you first passed away. And you stay that age forever.

Perpetual age has its pros and cons, but it all depends on what that age is. Being turned during your teens results in retaining a youthful innocence while allowing you to mentally mature. You stay looking young but get wiser as the years go on. A young physical appearance causes a problem, though: anything that requires you to be an adult remains a challenge. You may be a mature adult at heart, but you'll still have to pay creepy, morally questionable dudes to buy you booze. On the

13. There can be only one! Unless, of course, it's replayed four more times that same day.

other hand, retaining your youthfulness with a wiser mind can have its advantages. Just imagine going back to high school with years upon years of experience in seduction. You can be a huge pedophile and nobody would know (figure 15).

As an adult, the possibilities really open up. You can't pose as a young kid anymore, but you're no longer limited to age restriction. This makes hunting for victims much easier and, most of the time, more enjoyable. The early twenties is generally the most desirable age range to stay around; you

Figure 15. Edward Cullen likes 'em young.

Figure 16. Little Johnny is never picked for baseball because he's a vampire, not because he's a scrawny dweeb.

retain your youthful good looks, but you don't stay too young. It's like college for the rest of your life! And we all remember what college was like.[14]

The extremes are where it gets the most problematic. Being turned as a young child is probably the toughest to deal with. For the rest of your life, you'll be stuck in a small child's body, never able to grow up and experience adulthood.[15] As a kid, this may seem fine, but once you mature you realize what you're missing: fully descended testicles.

That and the ability to have sex. If you never hit puberty, you can't expect your junk to work. And as if a life without experiencing sex wasn't bad enough,[16] just imagine spending an eternity with a fear of cooties. Not to mention a lifetime of being the subject of unrestrained childhood ridicule (figure 16).

14. Some "experimenting" I'd rather not talk about.
15. Contrary to popular belief, being a Toys "R" Us kid really loses its appeal after a few years.
16. Just ask my World of Warcraft guild master.

The other end of the spectrum isn't much better, either. From around sixty-five and on, you're stuck in the body of an old person. It's basically a never-ending early bird buffet line. A perpetual state of never going above fifty on the freeway. Everlasting bingo binges and dinner at three in the afternoon. An eternity of *Murder, She Wrote* reruns and uncontrollable bowel movements. Adult diapers.

Invulnerability

Invulnerability goes hand in hand with immortality. Since conventional weapons don't hurt vampires, they become invulnerable to most physical and biological attacks. The attacks still harm them, but the effects don't last very long. The key to this type of invulnerability is their superior ability to regenerate. If a human were to cut his or her arm, for example, it could take weeks to fully heal. For vampires, it would heal in a matter of seconds.

It should be noted that vampires still feel pain, though. Their wounds heal much, much faster, but the initial pain is still very much present. Contrary to what some movies may have shown, no vampire is capable of casually walking around with a barrage of bullets showering into them. The force of the bullets alone makes that impossible, not to mention the pain threshold involved. Ever been paintballing? It hurts like a bitch. They only bruise you, but they'll still make you crawl into a fetal position while multicolored death rains down upon you.

In addition to physical attacks, vampires are also completely immune to every human disease and illness known to man. Cancer, AIDS, gingivitis—all have zero effect on vampires. Experimentation has been done in attempts to replicate this ability in humans, but so far all attempts have been unsuccessful.

With the number of deadly, incurable diseases plaguing humanity today, complete immunity is a very appealing aspiration. Some have suggested allowing the terminally ill to be turned into vampires as a cure for their illnesses. Under a highly controlled government program, this could feasibly be possible. However, we can barely get marijuana legalized for glaucoma treatment. Vampirism wouldn't go over too well with government officials.

No Reflections

One of the more unique and scientifically interesting abilities in the vampire arsenal is their lack of a reflection. With the naked eye, vampires can be seen just as easily as a normal human being. However, when vampires step in front of a mirror, it's like they're not even there. They can't be seen in the mirror at all. The cause of this has yet to be determined, but a popular hypothesis involves the unique way their incredibly pale skin refracts light.

This ability, while limited in its use, definitely has noticeable pros and cons. On one hand, it makes sneaking up on people in the bathroom a whole lot easier, but it also prevents them from using mirrors themselves. Which brings up the question: How do vampires do their hair so well?

One would think not having a reflection would make it difficult to do your hair, but those perfect hairdos of theirs are pretty amazing. So amazing, in fact, that you'd almost think "never having a bad hair day" was another special ability of theirs. It's mind-boggling how they can get such flawless hair when they can't even see themselves. Just look at blind people.[17] Hairstyling disasters.

Super Strength

The idea of super strength is a little misleading. Vampires never acquire superhuman strength at all, nor do they increase their strength just by being turned into a vampire. In fact, vampires have the same strength they had as a human. At least to begin with.

This "power" is actually, once again, based on their regenerative abilities. Their ability to heal so quickly allows their muscles to grow exponentially faster than a human's. Regular muscle growth is caused by engaging in rigorous exercise that harms your muscles and then allowing them time to heal and grow. Rather than having to wait days for muscles to heal, like humans do, vampires are able to heal almost immediately. They still require training and diligence, but the turnaround is a lot quicker.

17. It's okay to stare; they can't tell when you're doing it.

Diet also plays a big role in overall fitness. Vampires often treat themselves to fancy food and fine wine, but solely as an act of pleasure, never for sustenance. The only thing vampires need to survive is blood. Most vampires, however, like to indulge. Because of this, it's not uncommon to see grossly overweight vampires. They may be immune to diabetes and heart attacks, but come on, get some control, guys (figure 17).

The "Vampire Diet," drinking only blood and consuming nothing else, is better than Atkins, South Beach, and Jenny

Figure 17. Vlad the Inhaler.

Craig combined.[18] When all you consume is blood, your fat and carbohydrate intake is zero. Plus, it's a lot of protein, which helps in building muscle.

Another "super strength" attribute vampires have, un-related to regeneration, is their massive bursts of adrenaline while under pressure. For example, if a female vampire's child was somehow trapped underneath a bus, her maternal instinct would immediately kick in. With a massive adrenaline rush, she would miraculously be able to lift the bus and save her child.

Increased Sexuality

The nice physiques (nonfatty) vampires inevitably get over the years can make for quite a powerful sexual attraction. This purely physical attraction is nothing compared to the innate increased sexuality vampires gain, though. This in-creased sexuality, a supersexuality, if you will, gives vampires the ability to attract almost anybody. Plus, they look great in black leather.

The primary function of this ability, aside from having awesome vampire threesomes, is seducing victims. Sure, vam-pires could just attack their victims and overpower them with their superior strength, but that method gets old pretty fast.

---

18. Following all three diets simultaneously would actually make you fatter. It's like when I tried to quit smoking. I used the patch, chewed the gum, and ate a ton of cold turkey all at the same time. It just made me more addicted. And sick of tur-key.

As immortals, they have to find new victims on a continual basis for all eternity. Might as well make that process enjoyable. So instead of just attacking a drunken bum in a dark alley, vampires head out to the hot spots at night, looking not only for a new victim, but sexual conquest as well. They make a game out of it.

With the influx of vampires in popular nightlife, it's becoming harder and harder for normal guys to find a partner. Even without the super attraction, male vampires get along with women much better than normal men. Hell, they even enjoy the menstrual cycle. Normal guys don't stand a chance.

Stretch Armstrong–Like Elasticity

Ladies . . .

Vampires > Zombies: Ultimate Powaaahhh

Vampires sure have a lot of cool powers. If I had to pick my favorite one, it'd probably be between super strength and immortality. With super strength you could do some crazy stuff like lift people's cars and junk, but with immortality you never die, which is awesome. But what do zombies have? A super ability to have bad skin and smell really bad? Gross.

Time Travel

Vampires don't have an innate ability to time travel. Nobody does. The bending of space and time is an immensely advanced level of physics that nobody today has even come close to mastering. In the very distant future, however, the puzzle has been solved and the technology for traversing through time has been created. And vampires have complete control of it.

Based on the reports of all recorded accounts of time-traveling beings, they all seem to fall under two categories: vampires and robot vampires. Because of this, I think it's safe to assume that in the future the human race will be reduced to near extinction and vampires will take over.

With the knowledge that the human race is pretty much screwed, you can stop worrying about the future and the environment and stuff. If we're not going to be there to enjoy it, no reason to give a shit anymore, right?[19] Or could this new-found apathy be the catalyst for the vampires gaining control? Could the future dictate how the past affects it? The present would have to start the process first, though, right? For that to work, the present would have to first affect the future, which then changes the past, which is really our present, to change our future, which is their present, which would change their past, our present, to change our future, their past, to affect

---

19. The human race: always looking out for number one.

their present, which would become our future. Okay, that makes sense.

Gaydar

Gaydar, or "gay radar," is the intuitive ability to gauge a person's sexual orientation or sense the presence of a nearby homosexual. It's like with Spiderman. You could just sort of tell he was gay.

Gayness, the flamboyant vibe that all homosexuals give off flows out of the body and resonates throughout the surrounding

Figure 18. Gayness looks like curvy arrows.

atmosphere. Many humans are able to intuitively detect gayness via sexual receptors, allowing them to "feel" this oscillating fabulousness (figure 18).

Vampires, with their heightened sexuality, pick up on this much easier than any normal human. Plus, it takes one to know one.[20] This "super gaydar" allows them to seduce only people who they know could be interested, making the hunting process much more efficient.

Teleportation

Limited, short-range teleportation is one of the more visually appealing abilities vampires have. Within a radius of about fifty feet, vampires are able to teleport objects, organic or otherwise, from one point to another. However, this ability is usually confined only to cages of doves and attractive, female stage assistants.

Mind Control

Through verbal cues and hypnotic suggestion, vampires are able to induce a state of hypnosis into unsuspecting victims. This allows them to feed without the victim putting up a struggle or creating unwanted attention. It also allows them to make their victims cluck like a chicken in front of all their friends. How embarrassing!

Reports have shown that once a victim is attacked it takes

20. "Dude, I think he just called us gay."

little to no concentration to control the victim. Really? So you don't need to do anything to the dude whose neck you just bit off to prevent him from fighting back? I never would have guessed.

Anti–Swamp Ass

Vampires have no sweat glands. Because of this, they are able to sit in a stationary position for extended periods of time without their butts getting all sweaty and gross.

Laser Eyes

They can also shoot lasers out of their eyes.

7. Misconceptions

The modern concept of the vampire, while initially based on truth, is still very far from it. Over the years, popular misconceptions have become more and more a part of the "common knowledge." What results is an odd mixture of truth and fiction. The biggest proponent of these inaccuracies is the film and entertainment industry.

Hollywood takes a lot of artistic liberties when it comes to vampire films. For dramatic effect, filmmakers will stretch the truth to hype up the story. Factual storytelling is bent, sometimes immensely, in the interest of making a more entertaining film. The end goal is to make money, so of course they are going to pander to their audience. Plus, how else do you think they were going to work all that nudity in and still have it be believable?

A good example of this is Mel Gibson's *The Passion of the Christ,* which depicts the events surrounding Jesus's crucifixion. What Gibson presents on the screen is way more intense than what really happened (see figure 19, next page).

These misconceptions play off the gullibility of others.

Figure 19. "Watch your step."

One person says something and it just builds from there.[21]
With enough time, these rumors become the truth to the misinformed public. Factor that into the misinterpreted actions
of vampires and you get a plethora of misunderstandings.

21. Did you hear? That nerdy kid from *The Wonder Years* is totally Marilyn Manson.
And he had surgery to remove his lower ribs so he could go down on himself! It's
totally true, dude!

Such erroneous beliefs can be extremely harmful. Not only do they perpetuate a more fantasized version of the vampire, but they also hinder our ability to protect ourselves. Just imagine somebody running home from a vampire thinking they're safe because vampires can't enter a house without being invited first. Sure, they may have impeccably high standards of courtesy, but that's not going to stop an impassioned vampire from catching his or her prey. That misinformed victim is as vulnerable as a blackout-drunk freshman chick at a frat party.

Kill the Leader, Free the Rest

Somewhere down the line, a myth began about killing the "original vampire" to break the curse. The idea is simple: killing a vampire would change every vampire he or she has turned back into humans. As if there was some supernatural bond between them or something.

This is completely false.

Killing a vampire to break the curse of whom he or she has turned, whether that vampire is the original one or not, has no effect at all. There's not even a curse to break; it's all physiological. You don't kill the hooker who gave you herpes to get rid of yours, do you? No, you don't. You can kill her because she gave it to you, but it won't have any effect on yours at all.[22]

---

22. Massive amounts of research have been done on this, resulting in nothing more than numerous dead hookers.

Flight

One of the more widely believed misconceptions about vampires is their ability to fly. Many believe that, like Superman, vampires can propel themselves through the air by some sort of invisible force. This is just not the case. Superman-like flight, a fluid movement through the air, is gravitationally impossible. It's simple physics. Flight requires propulsion. Simply sticking your arms out in front of you doesn't create propulsion of any kind. Well, except for the propulsion toward getting your ass kicked for acting like a moron.

This myth of flying most likely started from witnessing a vampire leaping over a wall or something. Their increased strength allows them to jump incredibly high. This ability, commonly referred to as "mad hops," can easily be misconstrued as flight.

Bats

As if the ability to fly wasn't preposterous enough, morphing into bats is even more ridiculous. There may be some mysticism surrounding bats and vampire culture, but the connection stops there. Vampires are entirely unable to change into bats, or any animal, for that matter. There's no shape-shifting at all.

The association between vampires and bats was most likely started with the discovery of vampire bats. Not only do they just so happen to share the same name, but vampire bats, like actual vampires, subsist by feeding on blood. The correlation between the two was obvious.

These specific types of bats are found only in Central and South America. Coincidentally, from those same areas comes the myth of El Chupacabra, a mysterious beast known to kill and drink the blood of farm animals, goats especially. The literal Spanish translation of *chupacabra* is "goat sucker." Whether this is a reference to vampires or Mexican donkey porn, we don't know for sure. We do know that sucking the blood of goats instead of humans is a major step down. Having sex with goats instead of donkeys, however, is just as gross.

Also of note, Batman is not a vampire, just some rich, gadget-obsessed asshole with a superiority complex. Nice cape, dick.

Sleeping Habits

Vampires are often depicted in movies and TV sleeping in coffins or hanging upside down. The idea of sleeping in coffins most likely came from witnessing a vampire rising from the grave for the first time. Actually sleeping in a coffin, though? No vampire does that. It's extremely uncomfortable. They don't make Posturepedic mattresses for coffins.[23] Plus, it's super claustrophobic in there.

Hanging upside down to sleep probably comes from vampires' connection to bats. Real bats hook their talons into

---

23. With viscoelastic memory foam! Originally made for astronauts!

cave ceilings and sleep upside down. The only time vampires sleep upside down is when they buy those special boots with hooks on them so they can hang upside down in their closets in hopes of stretching their bodies out to get taller. Very few do this, though.

The Goth Scene

The misguided connections between vampires and Goths have run rampant for centuries. The two groups have a couple of similarities, so the association is obvious.

The original Goths were a group of East Germanic tribes who adopted Arian Christianity[24]—an entire horde of sad, lonely people. Like the Goths, vampires also have a very strong eastern European background.

Present-day Goths often wear lots of black clothing, like those huge baggy pants with an abundance of unnecessary bullshit hanging from them. Or trench coats in the summer. Vampires also wear lots of black, although they do it because it makes it easier to sneak up on people at night.[25] Plus, it's slimming.

Because of these connections, vampires and Goths tend to get grouped together quite often. However, for the most part, vampires aren't into the Goth scene at all—a characteristic they share with most humans. In fact, most vampires despise

---

24. Not to be confused with Aryanism. Goths aren't racist. They hate everybody, including themselves, equally.

25. That's just dangerous. Walking around at night in dark clothes? You could get hit by a car! Didn't you listen to your mother? Shame on you.

being connected with Goth culture, especially with the music scene. Have you ever listened to Goth music? Vampires are undead, not deaf.

Truth be told, there are actually more Dave Matthews Band vampire fans than Goth vampire fans. And I'm talking big fans, as dedicated as any other Dave Matthews Band fan is. Dudes who wear socks with sandals, who are perpetually stoned, and refer to the band as "Dave." Just total hippies.

Feed Three Times

Some believe that in order to turn a human into a vampire, another vampire needs to feed from that person a total number of three times. The basic flaw with this can be seen with simple science. The act of feeding is not any kind of mystic ritual. It's simple fluid transmission—like from a snakebite or physical contact with a prostitute. It's a onetime deal.

It's not like they need to take a certain amount of blood, either. As if they always take the same amount each time and need to feed three times to take enough.

Of course, there is an even more major flaw: What idiot would let himself or herself be attacked by a vampire three times? After the first attack, you'd feel lucky to still be alive. After the second attack, though, you'd start taking precautions against another attack. Only an idiot would willingly allow it to happen again. Sure, there are unwilling victims, but it's not like all vampires are sadistic psychopaths who capture their victims and hold them against their will. These are vampires, not Ted Bundy.

Messy Eaters

Visual depictions of vampires caught in the act of feeding often reveal blood smeared all over their faces and splattered across their clothes and the victim. Are vampires just messy eaters by nature? Not in the slightest. Most are actually

Figure 20. AWESOME!!

quite clean. A large number of vampires actually practice table manners akin to those followed during the Victorian era, sometimes compulsively so. It's not uncommon to see a vampire sucking blood while holding a pinky out.

So if they aren't messy eaters, why the messy theatrics? The answer is simple: dramatic effect. Popping your head up from a freshly slain victim, your mouth covered in blood, and letting out an evil hiss is enough to scare off any unsuspecting bystander (figure 20). Plus, it just looks so cool!

Vampires > Zombies: I Think I Can, I Think I Can

Okay, so vampires can't really fly or turn into bats, but you know what they can do? Show emotions, make decisions, have cognitive thoughts, etc. Zombies are incredibly stupid. No, they're beyond stupid. Hold out your chainsaw while one is running toward you and what'll it do? Run right into it and die. Morons.

A Numbers Game

It may come as a surprise, but there are a large number of people throughout the world who still don't believe in vampires. These people, usually scientists,[26] completely reject the existence of vampires. Two such nonbelievers, physicists

26. Ugh, I know, right?

Costas J. Efthimiou and Sohang Gandhi, even went as far as publishing a paper to disprove the existence of vampires. Using math. That's the first red flag right there: two physicists trying to use math.

The paper, entitled "Cinema Fiction vs. Physics Reality: Ghosts, Vampires and Zombies" (last revised August 27, 2007), attempts to, in the span of a mere two pages, mathematically disprove the existence of vampires.

These physicists' major flaws start right at the beginning, where they make several unfounded assumptions.

The first assumption is of the average vampire's feeding frequency, which they arbitrarily set at once per month. They've chosen this number because when compared to any Hollywood vampire film it's a highly conservative assumption and only a fraction of the frequency commonly depicted. To translate to laymen's terms: they pulled this number out of their ass. Coincidentally, however, it seems they made a lucky guess.

Most vampires feed, on average, once every twenty-eight to thirty days, making their assumption correct. This doesn't justify their method of getting to this number, though. Making a complete guess based on nothing but cinematic depictions has absolutely no scientific basis. Facts based on what you've seen in the movies? I am personally appalled anyone would even consider doing such a thing. Shame on you.

Efthimiou and Gandhi also assume that no vampire ever dies and every attack results in the victim becoming a vampire himself or herself. Neither of these assumptions is true, but let's assume they are for a moment. With a feeding frequency of once per month, the vampire population would grow at an exponential rate. This rate of growth is what Efthimiou and Gandhi use to disprove vampire existence.

Every vampire attack results in the vampire population increasing by one and the human population decreasing by one. Based on this idea, Efthimiou and Gandhi present us with their super vampire population equation:

$$2 \times 2 \times \ldots \times 2 = 2^n$$
Math!

Look out! That's basic high school algebra! Assuming we start with a single vampire, the "equation" gives us the number of vampires after n months have passed. Based on this, Efthimiou and Gandhi conclude that the minimum time it would take to exterminate the entire human population is thirty months. They then determine that vampires cannot exist because their existence contradicts our own.

Many[27] experts[28] consider this undeniable proof that vampires don't exist. Remember, though, this is based on several assumptions.

The human population in their example only ever changes when a vampire attacks a human and turns that person into a vampire. Human reproduction is never taken into account.

27. One.
28. Blogger.

China alone could repopulate the rest of the world in, like, a week and a half.

The key issue with their argument is the growth of the vampire population. The example assumes that not a single vampire dies during those thirty months. In the real world, vampires die all the time, for a multitude of reasons, such as these:

- Vampire Slayers (more information available in Chapter 11, "The Thrill of the Hunt").
- Vampire-on-Vampire Crime: It's not uncommon for a vampire to kill another vampire. They did used to be human, after all.
- Suicide: No, it's not because they're emo. Recently turned vampires are often reluctant to kill another animal, human or otherwise,[29] in order to live. Others are simply unwilling to accept life as a vampire.
- Accidents: Whether it's accidentally walking outside in the sun or tripping and falling on a stake, accidental death is not rare in the vampire world. Clumsy idiots get turned every now and then, too.

The biggest proponent of keeping the vampire population in line is the bureaucracy of covens. Covens are tight-knit groups of vampires who act almost as families. These families follow strict rules and regulations when it comes to feeding. They store fresh blood year-round to lower the number of people they must attack. More importantly, they rarely ever let their victims turn.

These rules ensure that the vampire population stays as

---

29. Vegans don't stand a chance.

constant as possible, as well as minimizes the negative effect on the human population. But what about the vampires outside of the covens?

In the wild, most predator species are outnumbered by their prey. If the feeding grounds get too crowded, the predators often turn on each other. If vampires outside of the covens get out of hand and refuse to follow the rules, the coven leaders simply have them killed. It's like a bureaucratic form of predator versus prey population control (figure 21).

Figure 21. Predator versus prey.

With these major factors dramatically stunting the growth of the vampire population, you can see the geometric progression in Efthimiou and Gandhi's example is nothing more than a bunch of bullshit.

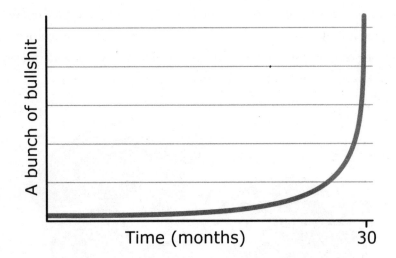

The mathematically based eventual extinction of the human race becomes impossible, and thus, their dismissal of the existence of vampires invalid.

QED, bitches.

8. Vampiric Behavior

Skeptics worldwide have discounted the existence of vampires for centuries. They remain unconvinced even with the thousands of reports and firsthand accounts of vampiric behavior. Some people, rather than ignoring it, chose to rationalize this behavior by equating the actions with existing human conditions. However, these are nothing more than superficial explanations.

It's like when stupid kids are wrongly diagnosed with attention deficit disorder. While the explanation may seem plausible, it's unreasonable to just disregard it based on a similarity. ADD could very well be the reason your kid isn't doing well in school, but he's probably just dumb.

These explanations aren't reason to completely discount the existence of vampires. They are, however, reason to scrutinize the validity of the reported sightings. Most people are stupid and extremely gullible. When misplacing their keys is reason enough for them to believe they're being haunted by ghosts, we need to take into account the possibility that they're wrong.

Allergies

It's a widely known fact that vampires are repelled by garlic. Skeptics attribute this feature to the human characteristic of allergic reactions. They propose that all accounts of vampires being repelled by garlic were actually just normal people having intense allergic reactions. Sure, guys.

For humans to have a severe reaction, they would have to consume a large amount of garlic in a short period of time. Doing so would cause gastrointestinal problems, rashes, and exacerbated asthma symptoms.

So if these recorded accounts of vampire attacks weren't actually encounters with vampires, then the crazy guy trying to murder someone must have left his inhaler at home and was afraid of getting a tummy ache.

Rabies

Humans contracting rabies is rare in developed nations like the United States, but in other parts of the world it can be much more common. Does this mean democracy prevents rabies? Yes. Yes, it does.

Rabies may not be common in urban areas, but it is still used to rationalize accounts of vampiric behavior. The symptoms of rabies include foaming at the mouth, hypersensitivity, and brain disturbance, each of which gets twisted around to explain reports of vampiric behavior.

When foaming at the mouth occurs, it is said that the

Figure 22. "It's okay! I have rabies!"

"foam" resembles blood. Rather than a vampire who has just recently fed, what is seen is just a rabies-infected person foaming at the mouth. Just like the person at his or her feet is "just sleeping" (figure 22).

Hypersensitivity affects reactions to sunlight and strong odors like garlic, while brain disturbances can cause abnormal sleep patterns, causing the infected to become nocturnal. But then again, so do hangovers. These may be plausible explanations, but they are ultimately invalid.

Snaggleteeth

The most prominent visual feature of a vampire is his or her fangs. Their main purpose, of course, is for piercing the skin of a victim to suck the person's blood. They also double as a great intimidation factor. Skeptics write this off as "dental irregularities," saying individuals with "fangs" are nothing more than normal people with overly prominent canines.

Even the snaggliest of snaggleteeth don't come close to a real vampire's fangs. Just look at popular American singer-songwriter Jewel. Scary, sure, but definitely not a vampire.

Cutaneous Porphyria

Science has tried to explain vampirism for ages, hypothesizing diseases and viruses as possible explanations for the changes in the human body when turned. One prominent example is cutaneous porphyria, a rare genetic disease that while not communicable (and thus unable to be transmitted through being bitten) displays effects that are very similar to vampiric behavior.

Those infected with cutaneous porphyria suffer from skin photosensitivity. When exposed to sunlight, their skin will get red, swell, and blister. Not quite bursting into flame like an actual vampire, but the similarity is clear.

In order to go outside, sufferers of this disease have to deal with the effects in several distinct ways. To protect their faces, sufferers wear an abundant amount of thick, white makeup with lots and lots of eye shadow. They are also forced to grow their hair long and wear lots of black clothing (preference to hooded capes) to cover the rest of their skin.

Treatment for this disease is strikingly more similar. It's not a cure, but intravenous heme is often used to suppress the effects. While blood transfusions are the usual course of action to get this, the same effect can also be obtained by consuming large amounts of blood.

Drug Use

One of the more peculiar sets of explanations for vampiric behavior comes in the form of drug use. Drugs have varying effects on the human body. Many of these effects are oftentimes used to explain vampiric behavior. Some skeptics have equated reports of vampires with a multitude of drug-related conditions, sometimes multiple conditions simultaneously.

For example, with their regenerative abilities, vampires are able to sustain multiple gunshot wounds with no negative effect. However, it could have just been some guy on PCP.

Many of the popular characteristics and abilities of a vampire can be explained through drug use. Again, of course, these are ultimately superficial explanations. The single fact that one would have to take all these drugs simultaneously to exhibit all the characteristics at the same time is reason enough to discount this hypothesis. Aside from the guys in Mötley Crüe, no human is even close to being capable of using such a combination of drugs and surviving.

Eating Habits

Have you never seen your neighbors eat normal food? They could be vampires. Or just on a meth bender and too busy tweaking out to be bothered with eating. If that's the case, the blood around their mouths is probably just due to their horrible oral hygiene.

Supersexuality

When confronted by an overly sexual person there's a good chance he or she is a vampire. Unless you're at a rave, in which case the person is just rolling on Ecstasy.

Super Strength

As previously mentioned, vampires' super strength is just an abnormal increase in normal human muscle development. This development is about on a par with steroid usage. If that's the case, the crazy demeanor of what is thought to be an attacking vampire is just "roid" rage.

Nocturnal Nature

Vampires are nocturnal creatures due to their inability to stay out in sunlight. Because of this, they only go out at night and stay inside and sleep all day. Frequent cocaine use often results in this same behavior.

Marijuana Usage

Vampires are just super chill, man.

Spontaneous Combustion

When exposed to sunlight, vampires practically explode in a ball of fire. And sometimes normal people just burst into flame.

Spontaneous human combustion is extremely rare, but it has claimed the lives of a number of people. There is no confirmed explanation for spontaneous combustion; the lack of any external source of ignition leaves the door wide open for speculation.

Many believe that there actually was a source of ignition and it was just mistaken for being spontaneous. Hell, it even could have been one of those monks protesting something by lighting himself on fire!

Hypersexuality

Hypersexuality is a controversial concept of sexual addiction similar to an OCD-like compulsivity. Sufferers frequently engage in sexual acts and are unable to resist sexual urges. Apparently getting laid all the time is a bad thing.[30]

Many equate the heightened sexuality of vampires with this type of sexual addiction. Reports of overly sexual beings could be of vampires, but some people are just sluts.

Premature Burials

Due to misdiagnoses or a lack of medical knowledge, every so often a living person will be buried alive. These instances are usually limited to places where modern medicine is not practiced, like the jungles of South America, all over Africa, and Amish settlements.

When said persons wake up, they find themselves trapped in a coffin buried six feet underground. It goes without saying, but they're a little freaked out. What happens next can be best described as intense, claustrophobia-induced hysteria.

---

30. Don't hate the player; hate the scientists who say you have a mental disorder.

They will manically claw at and beat on their coffins in hopes of escaping. If they are able to get out, they emerge from the ground caked with blood and dirt, a sight any bystander would assume as someone returning from the grave.

To further this speculation, when such persons finally emerge from their grave, they have quite literally gone insane. Primitive instincts and revenge are the only things left running through their minds. If you were buried alive, you'd be pretty pissed off, too.

Vampires > Zombies: Doctor, Doctor!

While displaying behaviors such as these is nothing to be proud of, the zombie equivalents are much, much worse. Whereas vampirelike behaviors include rabies and being allergic to garlic, the zombielike equivalents include leprosy, the plague, and poor hygiene!

Cannibalism

Vampires don't eat their victims, but feeding looks a whole lot like it from afar. It's hard to distinguish one from the other. Because of this, skeptics write off accounts of vampires feeding on their prey as cannibalism.

Jeffrey Dahmer wasn't a vampire, but just because he ate people like a vampire doesn't mean that it can be considered evidence that vampires don't exist. It just means he was incredibly fucked up.

Immense Disdain for Christian Iconography

At the sight of a cross, vampires will reel back, horrified at the object in front of them. Skeptics like to attribute this behavior to overly dramatic atheists expressing their opinions in as showy a manner as possible. Just the sight of a cross or the inclusion of Jesus in their children's elementary school holiday performances gets them super pissed.

These theatrical displays of outrage may be a means to further their religious, social, or political agendas, but as far as we are concerned, all it does it make them that much more vulnerable. The fewer crosses around the more prone to vampire attacks you'll be. Perhaps they should worry about more pressing issues like staying alive, rather than arguing against calling the winter holiday "Christmas vacation" or not.

Section 3

Kill or Be Killed

9. Defending Yourself

With all the information we have on vampires and their abilities, defending yourself against attacks may seem like an overwhelmingly daunting task. Truth is it's not as intimidating as it may seem.

The best way to defend yourself against a vampire attack is to prevent vampirism altogether. Obviously, you can't do much to prevent vampires from turning other people, but you can prevent the dead from returning from the grave, a concept further discussed in Chapter 13, "Becoming One."

Such prevention is known as maschalismos, the practice of physically rendering the dead incapable of returning from the grave. This is achieved by the simple and not-gross-at-all task of cutting off various body parts such as the feet, hands, ears, and nose. Sure, Grandpa may have wanted an open-casket funeral, but some things just take priority over others.

This form of ritual mutilation is often practiced by serial killers as well. This is usually done in fear of their victims returning from the grave to seek their revenge. Other times it's just because most serial killers are sadistic psychopaths. Sometimes both!

Prevention, of course, can help only so much. Your best chance at survival is noticing a vampire before it's too late. You're in a much better standing if you spot a vampire before he or she attacks rather than afterward. Luckily, several tricks have been developed over the centuries to help with preemptive vampire detection.

Reaction to Fresh Blood

Like sharks, vampires smell blood and become immediately attracted to the source. They are almost subconsciously compelled to follow it. It's instinct.

Due to this instinctual reaction, if you have a feeling that someone is a vampire, you can cut yourself to draw blood and observe how they react (the only time cutting yourself is actually helpful).

Suits and Capes

It might not be very common anymore, but some vampires still dress in Victorian-era fashion. It's incredibly easy to just avoid these people altogether. Even if they aren't vampires, you generally want to steer clear of those freaks as well.

Not So Sly

Oftentimes, when seducing potential victims in clubs, the cockier vampires will use cliché pickup lines like "Your coffin or mine?" and "You can suck my blood any day." These corny lines are more than enough to tip you off against a possible vampire and/or douche bag.

When detection fails, you're left with nothing but the tried-and-true methods of physical deterrence. These come in several forms, the most popular of which come in the form of apotropaic items, objects intended to ward off evil. The most common of which is, of course, a crucifix.

Crosses and Crucifixes

The classic vampire deterrence, crosses and crucifixes serve as the easiest (and oldest!) method of keeping yourself safe from vampire attacks. You can't exactly carry around cloves of fresh garlic everywhere you go. Sure, it'll ward off vampires, but it'll ward off normal people at the same time. Except maybe Italians, but they're hardly normal.

What makes a cross so appealing is its ease of use. Wearing one around the neck is usually enough to ward off any vampire. Oftentimes, crosses are incorporated into the world of fashion. Spruced-up crosses, or "bling," become not only a means of warding off vampires, but also both a fashion statement and a status symbol (figure 23).

Figure 23. STRAIGHT FLOSSIN'.

Crosses may be great tools, but they aren't perfect. The reliability of a cross depends on the person using it and the strength of the attacking vampire. For example, it's possible for a relatively strong vampire to simply knock the cross out of the hands of its victim. Or if the cross is being worn around the neck, a vampire can make an initial attack from behind, using the person's body as a shield from the cross itself.

What a cross does bring to the table that no other deterrence can is its ability to double as a self-motivational tool. Scared and running for your life? Just look to your cross and ask yourself, "What would Jesus do?"[31]

Garlic

Dating back just as far as the use of crucifixes, garlic has also been a popular means of preventing vampire attacks. While hunting, vampires rely on a keen sense of smell to seek out potential victims. Hanging garlic on the doors and windows of your home is often enough to deter a vampire. Garlic's just that gross.

An even stronger use of garlic, however, is the actual consumption of it. Garlic is known to cause halitosis, also known as bad breath, or "stank mouth." As much as a vampire may want to feed, seducing a potential victim with bad garlic breath becomes a major turnoff.

---

31. Die and return from the dead.

Being Black

Vampires were being racist way before it was ever cool to do so. This history of racist vampires goes all the way back to Dracula, the biggest perpetrator of spreading racism. In the movie *Blacula*, for example, Dracula is asked to help suppress the slave trade in Africa and instead imprisons Blacula in a coffin for all eternity. What an asshole.[32] Even Brad Pitt's character in *Interview with the Vampire* had an entire plantation full of black slaves.

It should be noted that even during the heat of slavery very few black people were ever attacked. When they were, though, they were killed to ensure they didn't come back.[34]

There aren't a whole lot of well-known black vampires, either. Aside from Blacula, there's Blade (who's only half vampire) and that big dude in *From Dusk Till Dawn*. There's just nobody else worth mentioning.

A vast majority of vampires simply refuse to attack black people. Not being attacked is nice and all, but it still comes with the sting of racism. Of course, this is positive overall, though; the black community already has more than enough to worry about. Like crack and "The Man."

---

32. More like "cunt" Dracula.[33]
33. (That's probably the title of a porno film.)
34. Is it still murder if they're only considered three fifths of a person?

Bodies of Moving Water

In the next chapter, "To Kill a Vampire," we'll learn about the use of holy water as a means of dispatching vampires. To summarize, holy water acts like acid to a vampire, burning through and disintegrating every inch of a vampire it touches. Because of this, vampires have an irrational—although justified—fear of water.

This fear makes any source of water a deterrent against vampires in the off chance that the water has been blessed. Being chased by a vampire in the woods? Just wade across a river and you'll be safe. For all we know, that water could have been blessed due to a baptism upstream—a whole river of holy water. It's the same "better safe than sorry" line of reasoning used against drinking straight from a river: who knows how many animals have been pissing in the water upstream. You just don't drink it.

Vampires > Zombies: No Solicitors

So what if you wanted to get a vampire to leave you alone? There's a ton of options to pick from, some of which are easy to come by household items. That's pretty convenient. Now what if you wanted a zombie to leave you alone? You're screwed. They just keep banging on your door until they find someone else to go bother. So annoying.

Just Being Plain Gross

Sometimes, having bad enough hygiene can cause a vampire to not attack. In order to feed, vampires must get intimately close to sink their teeth in. Just imagine a vampire getting ready to bite your neck only to be met with a platoon of puss-filled boils and acne. It's like small-scale biological warfare!

This method of deterrence does come with the side effect of never getting a date again, though. It's probably best to consider your other options before jumping into using this one.

Other Deterrents

Aside from the aforementioned major deterrents, there is a collection of minor deterrents. These aren't much more than various peeves that make vampires angry, but when used in conjunction with one another (or, even better, alongside a major deterrent), they lower your chances of being attacked even more. Be careful, though; you do run a very high risk of becoming a douche bag depending on what combinations you choose. These minor deterrents include:

- Popped collars.
- Crying babies.
- Spray tans.
- Spoken-word poetry.
- Dogs in purses.
- Reality television.

- Rappers with "Lil" in their names.
- Rappers without "Lil" in their names.
- Deepak Chopra.
- People who buy porn at the airport.
- Bumper stickers that promote specific beliefs, like who you think we should be voting for in 1992.[35]
- Bathroom attendants who expect tips, as if making me uncomfortable by staring at me while I pee was a favor. Is it my fault I pull my pants all the way down?
- Techno music. Call me a musical elitist, but I like my music to not sound like two robots having a screaming argument with each other as much as possible. Especially if those robots are apparently inside an industrial warehouse clanging metal together. And those random air raid sirens, good Lord. I guess the warehouse is being targeted for a bombing raid to deal with the robot situation. Let's just hope all those police blowing their whistles get out in time.
- Ex-girlfriends.

35. Ross for Boss!

10. To Kill a Vampire

I think I should warn you all, when a vampire bites it, it's never a pretty sight. No two bloodsuckers go the same way. Some yell and scream, some go quietly, some explode, some implode, but all will try to take you with them.

—*Edgar Frog (*The Lost Boys, *1987)*

Deterrents are good for protecting yourself against attacks, but for a more proactive approach, you'll need something a little more offense oriented. Garlic and crosses help neutralize the threat, but only temporarily. Sometimes getting your hands dirty is your only choice.

There aren't many methods for dispatching vampires. Your choices may be limited, but the options are there.

Decapitation

Due to their regenerative abilities, normal physical attacks won't do much toward killing vampires. It may deter them for a while, but that's it. Killing a vampire through purely physical means is limited to destroying the connection between the heart and the brain. The most logical means of accomplishing that?

As French revolutionaries used to say, "Off with their heads!"

Or as Marie Antoinette would say, "Shit."

Decapitation can be nasty depending on the tool used. Luckily, there are numerous choices, including swords, chainsaws, guillotines, Rock 'Em Sock 'Em Robots, or even talking one's head off through incessant nagging.

Stakes

Rather than severing the connection between the heart and the brain, you can also just destroy either one. This is commonly done by piercing the organ with a stake.

The brain isn't exactly an easy target. The human skull is remarkably resilient and makes penetration almost as difficult as penetrating a virgin with strong moral beliefs waiting until marriage. The heart, however, is perfect.

A stake to the heart is the most traditional method of killing vampires. Contrary to what the legends may say, though, it doesn't have to be a specific type of wood, or wood at all, for that matter. You can even be ironic and use a Dracula action figure. Any sharp object will do. Anything can be used to stab a fool—just look at prison shanks.

Holy Water

Holy water, water that has been blessed by a priest, is extremely dangerous for vampires. When thrown on a vampire, it acts like acid; disintegrating everything it touches.[36]

Part of what makes holy water so great is its abundance. Obtaining holy water might not be the easiest task to accomplish, but once you have it your supply becomes infinite. Adding ordinary water to holy water blesses the entire supply. Serious vampire slayers will even go as far as becoming ordained so they can bless water themselves.

The real strength of holy water is its versatility; the number of ways to use it are innumerable. The obvious method, of course, is filling squirt guns and water balloons with it.[37] Slayers are an inventive bunch, though, and are known for getting pretty creative with holy water usage.

One such slayer, an ordained priest living in Alaska, is known for his quick thinking and use of holy water. Tales of this "arctic battle-priest" tell of his frequent use of his frozen surroundings. During one specific encounter, he was face-to-face with a vampire when he broke off a nearby icicle, blessed it, and drove it through the vampire's heart. How cool[38] is that?

---

36. H_2 Ohhh noooooo!!
37. Oh, blessed Super Soaker.
38. Pun intended!

Fire

Fire alone is unreliable; it usually goes out before it can kill a vampire. It leaves vampires nearly helpless, but still alive. With their regenerative ability, charbroiled vampires will be back to 100 percent in under a day's time. So use the opportunity to strike them while they're vulnerable and weak.

Poke them with sticks, mess with their hair (if they still

have any), call them names, make jokes about them[39] and eventually drive a stake into their heart.

Wet Willies

Wet willies (licking your finger, then putting it in someone's ear) can be incredibly deadly to a vampire. If done in front of enough people, the embarrassment and shame would be so overwhelming that the vampire would die right then and there.

Just make sure you lick your finger before putting it in the vampire's ear. Vampire earwax, if enough is consumed, works just like drinking their blood. Don't want to accidentally turn yourself into a vampire now. Plus, it's earwax. That's just gross.

Exposure to Sunlight

When exposed to direct sunlight or pure UV light, vampires burst into flames almost immediately. It's like when pasty, freckled, redheaded kids get sunburns but taken to a whole new level. Not even melanin can save them.

Aside from forcing vampires to spray tan, this physical reaction can be employed to exterminate vampires, either by physically forcing a vampire into sunlight or by using powerful UV flashlights. They're the only creatures who actually can have their eyes burned with laser pointers.

---

39. Oh, *Burn!*

Silver Bullets

Vampires are highly allergic to silver. This reaction is primarily due to its holy connotations, much like holy water. So once again, the atheists were wrong. Sorry, guys.

By using bullets made of silver, gunfire will inflict much more damage and cause a lot more pain to attacking vampires. Plus, a shot to the head or heart is almost a guaranteed kill. Silver bullets are also used against werewolves, witches, dragons, ninjas, bigfoots,[40] and several other "mythical" creatures as well.

So load up on silver bullets, hold that gun sideways gangsta style, and show them punk bitches who they messin' with.

Vampires > Zombies: Headshot!

There aren't a lot of ways to kill a vampire, but you still have your options. Sunlight especially makes it really easy. But zombies won't stop until you put a bullet in their head. You can light those assholes on fire and they'll still run after you. What a bunch of dicks.

To be 100 percent sure a vampire is dead, your best bet is to drive a stake through his heart, place a clove of garlic in his mouth, cut off the head, douse him in holy water, place the body in direct sunlight, and then scatter the ashes on opposite sides of the planet. If possible, sending some of the ashes into space is preferred, but not all of it. God forbid you're the cause of a superrace of space vampires.

---

40. Bigfeet?

11. The Thrill of the Hunt

All right, vampire killers . . . let's kill some fucking vampires.
—*Seth Gecko* (From Dusk Till Dawn, *1996)*

Vampire slayers are people who have dedicated themselves to the pursuit and killing of vampires. They are professionals, but only in the sense that they have mastered the techniques and skills required for the job. There's no certification in killing vampires. You can't go to the learning annex and take a course in vampire slaying.

Most old school slayers were Christians who believed vampires were servants of the devil and it was their duty to destroy them, much like what they did with Muslims during the Crusades. For others, the task was handed down by generation, as seen with the Van Helsing family. If that family knows anything, it's how to kill vampires and instill a vampire-hating determination in their kids. Thank God they weren't racists.

Slayers Today

Nowadays, those who dedicate themselves to pursuing and killing vampires are often shunned by their peers. Saying you hunt vampires doesn't exactly bode too well for social acceptance. Slayers also travel often and are thus usually unable to form any serious relationships should the opportunity even arise. This solitary lifestyle, along with its supernatural aspects, becomes extremely attractive to flocks of lonely nerds.

These desperate dorks actually come in quite handy when teams are being put together.

A slayer team works together as a cohesive group, hunting vampires in a more organized, militaristic fashion. These teams can range anywhere from duos to large group operations. Most consist of about five people and include a certain core of characters, each with a certain specialty:

- The fearless leader: Every team requires leadership, someone to plan attacks and make tough decisions. The leader is also usually a little bit of an asshole.
- The ex–military weapons expert: The resident gear head and gun nut. He has a short temper but bottles it up and takes it out on vampires.
- The chick: She has a rough exterior but secretly hides her feelings for their fearless leader.
- The computer/science nerd: He wouldn't stand a chance in a fight,

but he can make some awesome high-tech gadgets to help against vampires.

And the token black guy.

Slayer teams work a lot like orgies: you can get it done on your own, but everything is better with a few more people thrown into the mix. If those people aren't doing what they're supposed to, though, things can get pretty nasty.

Finding people with similar interests is hard enough. Finding qualified people is even harder. You can't exactly take an ad out in the newspaper. Craigslist is even worse. Out of all the people who reply, about 5 percent are generally interested, but underqualified. The other 95 percent are just guys sending in pictures of their dicks.

Slayer Team Needs Chick Member

Date: 2009-03-12, 10:32PM PDT

Our vampire-slaying team needs a female member!

As the team's leader, you will likely end up sleeping with me. Preferably be tall, blond, and leggy. Also, if you've got a hot friend to bring along that'd be cool.

No fatties please.

- Location: San Diego
- It's NOT ok to contact this poster with services.

Heigh-ho, Heigh-ho

Hunting vampires is an expensive way of life, especially considering the gear requirements and travel costs usually involved. For a job that you don't get paid for, it sure can be a big money sink. Without some sort of financial backing, you're forced to resort to other means of earning a wage. Blade, for example, steals from vampires before he kills them.

The equipment used by most slayers, while expensive, gives them a necessary advantage. Vampires aren't easy targets to hunt. Having the gear necessary for the job, possessing the training needed to be prepared for anything that may happen, and being on the offensive gives slayers a much needed upper hand.

Vampires > Zombies: Hunting Season

Hunting is supposed to be about the thrill of the hunt. Vampires are just as smart as you are and will do everything in their power to not get killed, making for an intense hunt. But zombies? There's no thrill when these retards just walk around aimlessly, waiting to get shot. Thanks for being boring targets, jerks.

Throughout the years, several slayers have earned names for themselves for being exceptional at what they do. Each does things a little bit differently, but they all do it well.

Buffy Summers

*I'm the thing that monsters have nightmares about. And right now,
you and me are gonna show 'em why.*
—*Buffy Summers (* Buffy the Vampire Slayer, *2003)*

Bio/History

Buffy is the eponymous vampire slayer, a status originally
held by Professor Van Helsing. Compared to Van Helsing,
Buffy is much more of a modern-era slayer—hip, young, and
not a weird, nerdy old man.

Buffy lives in Sunnydale, a small town in California.
In addition to dealing with the normal problems of high
school girls, like math and boys, she hunts vampires, monsters, and all sorts of other demons. Sunnydale had been a
haven for evil and the paranormal for quite some time, but
in an unfortunate twist of fate, a portal known as the Hellmouth opened up just after Buffy moved to town. Could this
be a simple coincidence? Is it fate? A weak plot device? Who
knows!

Luckily for her, she is often helped by a group of friends and
her watcher (a slayer-mentor of sorts), Giles. In a strange turn
of events—especially for a slayer—several of those friends actually become monsters themselves, including a werewolf and
a witch. She's even had multiple relationships with vampires.
Some see this as a double standard, but others see it as incredibly hot.

Weapons of Choice

Buffy may be a modern-age slayer, but when it comes to weapons, she keeps it old school with wooden stakes. On one hand, becoming proficient with stakes allows her to use virtually any sharp object as a weapon. On the other hand, dealing with splinters really sucks.

She also uses her good looks and schoolgirl charm to work for her. She is totally underestimated. Nobody expects a Valley girl cheerleader to kick his or her ass.

Famous Kills

The number of vampires Buffy has dispatched ranks in the hundreds. One particular vampire stands out: The Master, one of the oldest and ugliest vampires of all time. After he escaped from the Hellmouth, which is conveniently located right underneath the library Buffy hangs out in,[41] she threw him into the library, where he was impaled on a piece of wood. His body disintegrated to ash, leaving nothing but a skeleton behind. Buffy and her friends celebrated by dancing.

Blade

I have spent my entire life searching for that thing that killed my mother, and made me what I am. And every time I take one of those monsters out, I get a little piece of that life back.
—*Blade (*Blade, *1998)*

---

41. Nerd!

Bio/History

Blade's mother was bitten by a vampire while she was pregnant with him, right before going into labor. What she was doing strolling around alone late at night while nine months pregnant is beyond me. Good job at being careful and protective while super preggo, mom.

Due to these strange circumstances, Blade was born as a half vampire of sorts, retaining vampire strengths without any vampire weaknesses. He can even stay in the sunlight, a trait for which vampires call him "daywalker" and "asshole." Dracula, with his penchant for old-timey, subtle racism, also refers to Blade as "the black."

After his mother died giving birth to him, Blade set out on a crusade against vampires, killing every one he could find. To finance this little operation, Blade steals from vampires and the humans who help them. It may be the most efficient way to get the money he needs, and to reinforce negative racial stereotypes.

Weapons of Choice

Blade definitely has the most impressive arsenal of weaponry. Aside from stakes and the usual weapons, Blade's armory consists of a few go-to items.

For close-quarters combat, nothing beats Blade's acid-etched, titanium sword. Decapitations and stabs to the heart are cake with this thing. It even has a booby-trap-like device that unless disarmed, will jut blades out of the handle and into vampires' hands. Bye-bye, fingers.

Also useful for close-quarters combat is what he calls "vampire mace," an aerosol-propelled mixture of garlic extract and silver nitrate (vampire rape whistle not included).

The heavy hitter of all his weapons, though, is the modified MAC-10 automatic pistol with silver-tipped, hollow-point bullets filled with liquefied garlic. Again, an efficient means, but the racial stereotypes are cutting pretty close. At least he doesn't hold the guns sideways. They're still badass, though.

Famous Kills

Out of every vampire slayer to have ever lived, Blade's kill count is leaps and bounds beyond them all. His abilities allow him to find places where large groups of vampires congregate and clear the whole place out single-handedly. It's impossible to even begin counting the number of vampire ravers he's killed. What is it with vampires and dancing in nightclubs to bad electronic music anyways? Don't they have any other hobbies? Or at least better tastes in music?

One of Blade's more famous kills was that of Deacon Frost after Frost successfully gained the powers of the blood god La Magra. This isn't to be confused with La Migra, which only Mexican vampires should be concerned about.

The Frog Brothers

Death to all vampires! Maximum body count! We're awesome
monster bashers! The meanest! The baddest!
—*Edgar and Alan Frog (* The Lost Boys, *1987)*

Bio/History

The Frog Brothers, known individually as Edgar and Alan, are a pair of teenage brothers who have dedicated their young lives to exterminating vampires in their home town of Santa Carla, California.

Santa Carla doesn't have much to offer besides the boardwalk and shirtless, beefcake saxophone players. Locals actually call the place the murder capital of the world. Obviously, none of them have ever been to Venezuela.[42]

The Frog Brothers run the local comic-book shop, which doubles as their main source for vampire research. It's mostly just a cover. As they say, they're dedicated to a higher power.[43]

Weapons of Choice

The Frog Brothers' choice of weaponry is fairly low rent compared to that of most other slayers. Their main weapon of choice is nothing more than a simple wooden stake. They have been known to use squirt guns filled with holy water at

---

42. Contrary to what *CSI* might portray neither Miami, New York, nor Las Vegas even comes close, either.
43. Being poster boys for the failure that is growing up as a child actor.

times, though. They're also well versed in the use of quippy one-liners and precociousness.

Famous Kills

In 1987, a friend of the Frog Brothers asked them to help deal with a group of vampires that was harassing his family. The three of them snuck into the vampires' lair and with a stake to the chest extinguished one of the vampires in a violent burst. He was asleep at the time, but a kill is a kill!

To retaliate, the other vampires attacked the family's house later that night. At one point, the Frog Brothers were cornered by one of the vampires, but the family dog pushed it into a bathtub filled with garlic and holy water. They splashed some of the water onto its face first, though. Totally their kill.

Slayer

Live by the sword and help to contain
The helpless minds of you all
Die by my hand in pools of blood
Clutch yourself as you fall
Mindless tyranny, forgotten victims
Children slaughtered in vain
Raping the maids, in which they serve
Only the words of the Lord
Die by the sword
Die by the sword
—*Slayer (* Show No Mercy, *1983)*

Bio/History

Possibly the longest-standing and most well-known slayer team of all time, the aptly named Slayer was formed in 1981 in Huntington Park, California, a known vampire hot spot at the time. Today, the city is completely devoid of any vampire activity whatsoever.

The group was formed when guitarist/vampire hunter Kerry King met Jeff Hanneman while auditioning for another slayer team. The two recruited bassist/vocalist/vampire hunter Tom Araya, who had slain with King in the past. The last member, Dave Lombardo, was recruited after he met King while delivering pizzas.

The team is an unconventional one: it doesn't have a nerdy computer guy, a female, or a token black guy—just four bad-ass dudes. It also doesn't use any of the conventional weaponry of a normal slayer team, relying solely on the power of thrash metal.

Weapons of Choice

Slayer single-handedly opened up the possibilities for what can be used to kill a vampire. The four of them never used anything except their musical instruments—guitars, bass, drums and screaming.

Famous Kills

While not an individual kill, the method used is quite notable. Slayer is able to perform music so heavy that it compels the people around them to form mosh pits. The raw power of a Slayer mosh pit has laid waste to many over the years.

Abraham Van Helsing

Do I like vans? Please. "Van" is my middle name.
—Van Helsing (Van Helsing, 2004)

Bio/History

Abraham Van Helsing was a man of many talents, working as a professor, a scientist, a physician, a van enthusiast, and a monster hunter. He was chosen by the Catholic church to hunt down several well-known monsters, such as Dracula,

Frankenstein, Dr. Jekyll/Mr. Hyde, Harry and the Hendersons (yes, the family included[44]), the Smurfs, Alf, and various others.

Possibly the most interesting aspect of Van Helsing is his family lineage. His descendants all seem to inadvertently become vampire slayers as well. Fate must suck.

Such descendents include

<blockquote>

Captain Abraham Van Helsing, captain of a salvaging spaceship in the year 3000.

Robert Van Helsing, great-great-great-grandson of Van Helsing, following in his footsteps as a geeky professor.

</blockquote>

44. Aiding and abetting a monster is equally as punishable.

- Eric Van Helsing, an incompetent slayer trying to exterminate a family of vampires in Wales, living in a trailer with his son, Jonathon Van Helsing, after his wife, Mina Van Helsing, left him for an estate agent.
- J. Van Helsing, Van Helsing's son.
- J.'s son, Leyland.
- Lawrence Van Helsing, unknown relation.
- Lawrence's grandson, Lorrimar Van Helsing.
- Lorrimar's granddaughter, Jessica Van Helsing.
- Conrad Van Helsing and his son, Adam Van Helsing, who hunted the vampire who killed Conrad's brother.
- Peter Van Helsing, a cousin of Van Helsing's and an advisor for vampire slayers.
- Dr. Rachel Van Helsing, Van Helsing's granddaughter and once leader of a group of vampire hunters.
- Integra Hellsing, Bureau Director of the Hellsing Organization, a British government strike force against supernatural menaces.
- Michael Harris, great-great-grandson of Van Helsing, was the only person not to keep the same last name. He did, however, name his high school band "The Van Helsings."

Weapons of Choice

Although the main weapon Van Helsing used was a crossbow, he was quite fond of using vans to hunt vampires. Whether this was done to be ironic or if he actually had a purpose for using them we aren't sure. What use does a van even have against fighting vampires? Undercover reconnaissance from afar? Can he run them over in it? Does he lure them in with promises of candy and then viciously molest them? What's the reason?!

Famous Kills

Though not technically his kill, Van Helsing is indirectly responsible for the death of a movie critic who committed suicide after watching the 2004 movie *Van Helsing*. It was pretty bad.

Robert Neville

If anyone is out there . . . I can provide food, I can
provide shelter, I can provide security. If there's anybody
out there . . . anybody . . . please. You are not alone.
—*Robert Neville (* I Am Legend, *2007)*

Bio/History

Most recently portrayed by Will Smith's character in *I Am Legend*, Robert Neville was supposedly the last survivor of a vampirism epidemic. The government claimed that a new cure for cancer had mutated into a lethal virus. We know, though, that the scientists working on that cure were experimenting with vampire DNA, trying to transfer their immunities to humans. And look what happened. Thanks, science.

Neville, who just happened to be a U.S. Army virologist, spent his days working toward finding a cure.

Before Will Smith's portrayal of Neville, he was first brought

Figure 24. ". . . from my cold, dead hands!"

to the screen as *The Last Man on Earth* in 1964, starring Vincent Price, and then again in 1971s *The Omega Man*, starring ex-NRA president Charlton Heston. Heston shot the living crap out of those vampires.[45]

45. "Those damn, dirty vampires . . ."

Weapons of Choice

Neville had a buttload of guns. He was also a very strong supporter and defender of the second amendment (figure 24).

> A well-regulated Militia, being necessary to the security of a vampire-free State, the right of the people to keep and bear Arms, shall not be infringed.
>
> —Amendment II (*The Constitution*, 1787)

Famous Kills

Himself

Section 4

Living with Vampirism

12. Faking It

It goes without saying, but vampires are easily the most fashionable of all monsters. A number of different subcultures and groups from all around the world are influenced by the vampire style. For some, though, an influence of style just isn't enough. The whole idea of being a vampire is extremely desirable. However, as attractive as it may be, most people are unwilling to deal with the consequences of being turned into a vampire. So what do they do instead? They fake it.

Faking it is generally frowned upon, by vampires and humans alike, but it serves as a safe alternative to actual vampiric transformation. On a whole, these fake vampires tend to fall under three distinct categories.

Vampyres

The most common of the three categories, Vampyres are those who choose to act as if they are real vampires, even though they most definitely are not. Most of the mannerisms this group is known for have been adopted from modern cinema, such as wearing lots of black clothing and makeup, staying indoors during the day, and drinking blood. Now, wearing lots of black and staying indoors are basic lifestyle choiccs, but drinking blood is taking that choice to an entirely different (messed-up) level.

Things Vampyres Have Adopted from Real Vampires

- Black trench coats
- Black hair
- Black corsets
- Black eyeliner
- Black stiletto boots
- Minimal interaction with other people

Vampyres don't pretend to have any sort of craving for blood like actual vampires do, but they choose to drink blood anyways. You know, just for the hell of it. This brings up numerous severe health issues, which is why it's usually done only with a person's partner. During intimacy, the "aggressor" will delicately cut into the flesh of his or her partner and drink the blood from the wound. Coincidentally, murder scenes that follow these exact details have played out in over a dozen episodes of *Law and Order: SVU*. The aggressor's partner gains satisfaction from being cut into—a heightening of feelings of sorts, a mixture of pain and pleasure. It's also an act that legions of emotional teenagers perform, but for the opposite reason (figure 25).

This is usually done with a knife or another sharp object, but some people take the dentistry route to have fangs surgically attached to their teeth. I guess it makes it more authentic. Why this is considered to be a reason to refer to oneself as a vampyre, though, is

Figure 25. The pain is the only thing that's real.

unclear. Sounds more like an otherwise normal person with a freaky S&M and bloodplay fetish if anything.

Psychic Vampires

Also known as "psy-vamps," psychic vampires usually make no attempt to outwardly portray themselves as vampires. Instead, their "vampiric" behavior takes place on the inside. Whereas real vampires feed off blood, psy-vamps feed off the energy of those in close proximity to them.

Have you ever known somebody who, whenever you are around them, just seems to suck the life out of the situation? Some of those people believe they are psy-vamps, rather than accept that they're just boring, party-killing, unentertaining downers.

Drinking blood makes sense;[46] it's a lifestyle choice. But psychic powers? These people actually believe they have some sort of psychic ability? Nobody really believes in that silly hypno bullshit.

There's actually a perfectly logical explanation for believing in psychic ability: people are fucking stupid. These social outcasts have tried to unsuccessfully fit in for years. To deal with this, they turn to Goth culture. With its ties with the vampire world, they soon discover this idea of the psyvamp, and the rest is history. "Oh my God, that's totally me! I'm a vampyre!" You're an idiot. These people have found an excuse (other than their own personal responsibilities) for not fitting in and have attached themselves to the idea.

It's like self-diagnosis with WebMD. You go on perfectly fine and leave thinking you have osteoporosis and attention deficit disorder.

Energy Vampires

While not a real category, energy vampires are really nothing more than another classification for psychic vampires, a subset if you will. In fact, both groups are exactly the same save for one distinct difference.

Energy vampires seem to be completely unaware of what they are doing to those around them, oblivious to the effects they have on people. Psychic vampires, on the other hand, do it on purpose. What a bunch of jerks.

---

46. Well, not really.

Plane Crash Victims

This last category, the least common of the three, varies significantly in terms of creation. Vampyres and psy-vamps are created from social context, but plane crash victims (PCVs) are created from disaster and the resulting mental illness. This transformation usually takes place high in a mountain or on a deserted island somewhere when a plane that has suffered a severe technical malfunction crashes. The sole survivor is then left with nothing but a ruined plane hull, dead bodies, and no connection to civilization. To survive, the PCV is forced to feed on the bodies of the passengers.

To gain a better understanding of the slow mental degradation one suffers during a disaster like this, use the following timeline of an example plane crash and imagine yourself in the situation:

0h:0m   Plane begins boarding. You shove the rest of your Cinnabon into your mouth before entering.

0h:10m You notice both flight attendants are women in their midforties. Both have bleached-blond hair and copious amounts of makeup caked on top of their fake tans. You feel sorry for their vain attempts to hold on to their youth.

0h:20m Captain announces the plane will be departing shortly.

2h:12m Takeoff.

2h:27m Flight attendant announces peanuts will not be served due to an allergy of one of the passengers. You recognize the bullshit and stop feeling sorry for her.

3h:40m Technical malfunction.

4h:40m Pilot announces the malfunction.

4h:41m Flight attendants begin cleaning up fecal matter from various passengers' seats.

4h:56m Lone virgin onboard makes desperate plea to lose virginity before he dies. Elder flight attendant volunteers.

4h:57m Virginity traded for humiliation.[47]

5h:06m Total engine failure.

5h:08m Crash.

5h:47m You regain consciousness and find yourself washed up on a beach, facedown in the sand. You have miraculously not drowned while unconscious.

5h:50m Begin search for survivors.

5h:51m Finding no survivors, you make a fire and a lean-to for shelter using spare wreckage and palm fronds.

6h:30m It's now been 6.5 hours since you've had anything to eat. Contemplating your situation, you realize what you must do to survive.

6h:40m Feast upon the flesh of another human.

7h:12m Harvest leftovers.

8h:43m You find a volleyball and begin talking to it.

9h:17m You decide growing a beard might be pretty cool.

---

47. Premature ejaculation is all the more embarrassing at 30,000 feet.

10h:02m   Bedtime.

16h:30m   You wake up: "Morning, Wilson."

16h:42m   Hungry, you find a healthy-looking Asian guy. Again feast upon the flesh of another human.

17h:07m   You're hungry again. Feast upon the flesh of someone more filling.

18h:32m   You are attacked by the smoke monster!

19h:57m   Begin searching the plane hull for useful items.

20h:11m   Discover stash of airplane food! You do your best Seinfeld impersonation.[48]

20h:41m   Discard airplane food; feast upon the flesh of another human.

23h:04m   Rescue workers arrive!

23h:37m   Feast upon the flesh of the rescue workers.

Given these extreme conditions, one can see how such a person would go crazy. It starts with eating people for survival and ends with a man drinking blood and running around like an animal, snarling at the rescue workers who come to save him.

As it stands, it's hard to say if this is due to humanity's primal instinct or whether our fascination with monsters in popular media has anything to do with it, but active research is being done and progress is under way.

---

48. "What's the deal with airplane food?!"

Vampyres, Psy-Vamps, PCVs

To better differentiate among a vampyre, a psy-vamp, and a PCV, use this handy list of prominent characteristics with the differences each type displays.

CLOTHING:

Vampyres: trench coats

Psy-vamps: The X-Files "I Want to Believe" T-shirts

PCVs: tattered pants and blood-soaked beards

MUSIC:

Vampyres: Goth, death metal, trance

Psy-vamps: Final Fantasy soundtrack

PCVs: the sound of animals screaming

FEMALE MATES:

Vampyres: European

Psy-vamps: Asian

PCVs: cadaverous

FOOD:

Vampyres: red wine

Psy-vamps: single-serving microwave meals

PCVs: human flesh

CINEMA:

Vampyres: horror

Psy-vamps: anime

PCVs: snuff

HOBBIES:

Vampyres: going to raves, judging people

Psy-vamps: playing video games

PCVs: talking to blood-smeared volleyballs

BOOKS:

Vampyres: Twilight

Psy-vamps: Twilight

PCVs: Twilight

SEXUAL ACTIVITIES:

Vampyres: BDSM

Psy-vamps: masturbation

PCVs: necrophilia

Skip the Side Effects

Automatically affiliating oneself with either group isn't necessary to fake vampirism. There are a multitude of things one can do to pretend to be a vampire without actually becoming one. Since the people attempting to copy an already established fashion sense obviously lack a sense of personal style, the following list can be used as a starting point to your new found self. Just remember, you are unique, just like everybody else.

- Avoid light to keep a pale complexion.
- Act snobby toward everyone.
- Dress in all black.
- Learn an archaic European language.
- Have caps affixed to your teeth for fangs (plastic Halloween fangs will not cut it).

- Dye your hair black.
- Learn some magic tricks.
- Change your name to something mysterious and evil sounding.
- Become a Wiccan.
- Hiss whenever someone taps you on the shoulder.
- Overcome your fear of talking to girls.
- Develop a hatred of people who look like werewolves (sorry, Armenians).
- Learn how to properly apply eye shadow and fingernail polish.
- Experiment with bisexuality.

Vampires > Zombies: Fashion Scene

Whether you appreciate it or not, vampires are incredibly influential to the world of fashion. People are so enthralled by the idea of vampires that they go out of their way to dress and act like them. You've got to admit, they're definitely the best dressed of all the monsters out there.

Zombies, on the other hand, wear the same dirty, rotting clothes every day of the week. Take a career homeless guy, drag him through a compost heap filled with broken glass, and maybe you'll get close to the same effect. Get with the times, zombies.

13. Becoming One

Bulgarians generally believe that particularly violent or cruel sinners are apt to return from the grave as vampires. These sinners include thieves, arsonists, prostitutes, and gypsies.[49] This is partially true. The truth is, though, there are several ways one becomes a vampire.

Getting Bit

The most well-known method of becoming a vampire is, of course, being bitten by a vampire. This is an act commonly referred to as "siring." After being bit, the usual "incubation" time is around one to two days, but this can vary depending on whether the timing would be dramatic or not.

And yes, you must actually be bit. Skin must be broken and blood must be shed. Hickeys don't count.

---

49. Bulgarians are known for being notoriously racist toward gypsies.

Natural-Born Killers

Those who are "born" as vampires are human until they die, at which point they return from the grave. The requirements for such a transformation to take place still elude us to this day, but we do know of specific instances that seem to have higher chances than others.

Violent or cruel sinners are no more prone to returning from the grave than anyone else. The Bulgarians were actually right about gypsies, though. Most gypsies return from the grave as vampires.

Illegitimate children have been shown to return from the dead as vampires slightly more often than others, as well. It's been hypothesized that the sanctity of marriage actually helps protect against vampirism, just one more thing those greedy homophobes who keep voting against gay marriage want to keep for themselves. So you can thank them for all the bastard vampires running around, angrier than usual because they don't have dads.

Children who are conceived during a holy period are highly likely to return from the grave as vampires. That's why anal sex is encouraged during Christmas. This effort was actually promoted by the Catholic church using the short-lived slogan "Buttfucking for Jesus."

Conception also plays another role in vampiric transformation.

Interesting Intercourse

Being the sexual creatures vampires are, sex between a vampire and a human is not at all rare. As mentioned, vampires often seduce victims before attacking them. This often includes lovemaking. Victims are then attacked and either killed or turned into vampires—but this isn't always the case.

Vampires and humans falling in love may be rare, but it happens. This is heavily frowned upon by the covens, but love can be a powerful motivator. So can really awesome sex. It's kind of like a vampire version of *Romeo and Juliet* except instead of everyone dying at the end, half of them just sort of hang around because they're immortal.

The main problem with a vampire–human relationship is half-breed procreation, the conception of half-human/half-vampire offspring. This type of reproduction is definitely possible, but only with a male vampire and a female human. The covens make sure such a child is never born. The implications of such a birth could be astronomical, especially if the child is named "The Chosen One."

In addition to half-breed babies, the act of intercourse itself is capable of transmitting vampirism. Because of this, you need a whole different type of protection against vampires.

Drinking Vampire Blood

The consumption of vampire blood is the most interesting form of vampiric transformation. First of all, for this to even take place, a vampire must drain its own blood. With Vampires' rapid regenerative abilities, this becomes a serious pain in the ass.[50]

Vampires are notorious for choosing whom they let turn, so to go out of their way to turn someone in such an ostentatious manner usually indicates some level of significance.

The actual transformation itself takes place at a cellular level. The vampire cells attack the human cells the same way a virus spreads—like a bajillion microscopic vampire attacks all at once.

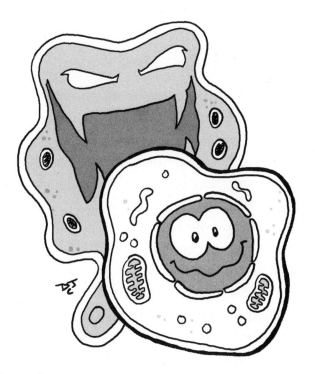

50. Quite literally so if they're trying to drain blood from their butt.

One would assume an alternative to getting bit would be preferable, but the cell-altering process is actually quite discomforting. It might not be as painful as being bit, but it lasts longer. Like ripping off a Band-Aid, it's best to do it quickly and just get it over and done with.

Toilet Transmission

Just like STDs, you can catch vampirism from public toilets. This begs the question: Why are people having sex with toilets in the first place? What are the logistics for that even?

Pop Rocks and Soda

There was an old urban legend that said consuming Pop Rocks and soda simultaneously would cause your stomach to explode and kill you. The legend was brought to the attention of the general public when Mikey, the cute little kid from the Life cereal commercials, became the most popular victim of this delicious death.[51]

There is a reason this is considered an urban legend: it's not true. In fact, Mikey never died at all. No exploding stomach or anything. He just got turned into a vampire.

Pop Rocks contain trace elements of vampire DNA. The popping sensation you feel when you eat them is actually the DNA interacting with your body. This works just like

51. "Hey, Mikey! He's dead!"

with the consumption of blood: vampiric transformation at a cellular level. However, in this case, such small trace amounts are no match for the human immune system. In fact, humans are completely incapable of consuming enough Pop Rocks to even come close to the amount needed for them to cause a threat.

This is where the soda comes into play. Carbonation acts as a "defense weakener" of sorts. Imagine Pop Rocks are an army of Vikings at the gates of a castle wall. Carbonation then is the battering ram used to break the wall down and let the soldiers in to rape and pillage.

The castle wall of the human body, in this case, is the lining of the stomach, mouth, and esophagus. Normally, the traces of vampire DNA are unable to penetrate this lining. Carbonation, though, weakens the lining and opens up pores that allow the DNA to flow right through and into the body. Let the cell rape commence.

Vampires > Zombies: Options!

Say you wanted to become either a vampire or a zombie. With vampires, you have several options to choose from, most of which don't even involve much pain. Even being bitten by a vampire isn't that bad if it's gentle enough. With zombies, you're pretty much stuck with getting mauled and eaten alive. Doesn't sound too pleasant, does it?

14. Life of a Vampire

Living as a vampire requires a decent amount of time to become accustomed to it. Avoiding sunlight at all times takes some serious getting used to.[52] Windows are often overlooked at first. Bullet holes in a wall can cause issues. Hell, buying the incorrect wattage for your lightbulbs can have devastating effects.

Let's not forget that never being in sunlight means you'll never be able to wear sunglasses without looking like an asshole.

Familiarization with this new way of life is never easy. There are innumerable new aspects and rules to take into account. What was once mundane as a human is now life-threatening as a vampire. Being scared of the dark just isn't an option anymore.

One of the harder aspects about life as a vampire is the job market. Feeding only on blood may negate the need to go grocery shopping, but money is still very necessary. Vampires have

---

52. Unless you're an antisocial hermit.

limited options when it comes to jobs they can take. There are a few types of jobs that bring extra benefit, though.

Life of Crime

Seeing as how the act of feeding is considered murder, a life of crime seems like an obvious choice for a vampire. Working as a contract killer or mugger allows a vampire to feed from his or her victims and earn money at the same time. You're killing two birds with one stone! And then drinking their blood!

Fit Right In

Few jobs allow vampires to be in close contact with humans without running the risk of being caught for what they really are. There are some jobs that let you fit right in, though. Working at costume shops, haunted houses, and Hot Topic stores is perfect. You just look like an enthusiastic employee.

We've Got What You Need

Some vampires are unwilling to take the life of another human. This makes feeding very difficult; however, some jobs provide an opportunity to amend that. Working as a blood bank attendee gives you access to a significant surplus of blood—blood that doesn't require killing anybody for.

Working at a morgue allows you to feed on fresh bodies that are already dead. A clean conscience and a full tummy!

Be careful, though. This isn't just taking home some office

supplies. Nobody will care when a few stacks of Post-it notes are suddenly missing, but people will definitely notice when a few bags of blood are gone or a corpse has some mysterious new wounds in its neck.

Vampires > Zombies: The "Living" Dead

Know what's cool about being a vampire? You can still have sex with people. And with those vampire seduction skills you'll be swimming in ass. Do you think you'd have as much luck if you were a zombie? Of course not.

The only possible people who could be into you would be necrophiliacs. Gross. And that's assuming you don't kill them first. You could always have sex with them afterward, though. You are already dead after all. Assuming sex between a zombie and a living human is necrophilia, what does that make sex between a zombie and a dead person? Does it stop being illegal and just become a weird fetish?

Obviously, all of these jobs must be relegated to only the night shift but they still provide a great benefit, especially with those that make feeding easier. Sucking blood is by far the most difficult aspect to get accustomed to. Nothing will prepare you for dealing with cravings and feeding for the first time.

Unless you used to be a cannibal as a human. Sicko.

Sucking Blood

The blood is the life.
—*Bram Stoker (* Dracula, *1897)*

Blood is a symbol of life. As a human, if you lose enough blood you'll die. Vampires subsist by feeding on the blood of the living, an act commonly known as hematophagy. This

Figure 26. "Mmmm . . . smooth."

feeding habit isn't unique to just vampires, either. Mosquitoes, worms, even Christians during communion all feed on blood (figure 26).

Vampires don't require the blood itself, just the hemoglobin contained in it. Not to be confused with one of Spiderman's archenemies, the Hobgoblin, hemoglobin is a protein contained in red blood cells. Vampires are unable to naturally produce hemoglobin due to a peculiar type of anemia and are thus forced to feed on others.

Luckily, feeding isn't a regular requirement. The doctor-recommended amount of blood to drink is approximately that of one average-sized person per month. This varies depending on the size of the vampire, of course.

Getting That Perfect Bite

As science has shown, the human body is full of guts. Knowing where to get that perfect bite can be a long and arduous game of trial and error if you don't know what you're looking for. The last thing you want to do is get a mouthful of slimy insides.

Studies of anatomy can show us where the most efficient and accessible areas to bite are located.

The Neck

As Hollywood will show us, the neck is by far the most popular place for a vampire to bite. But aside from getting a good reaction shot, why is this?

The neck is home to the carotid artery, which supplies blood to the head and neck. It is the largest artery in the human body besides the arteries in the heart. The blood flow and accessibility of this artery is second to none. It also allows you to take out the victim's vocal chords to prevent screaming. These same features are why assassins choose to go for the throat as well.

It should be noted that popping your collar has zero effect on deterring this type of attack against you. In fact, all this does is annoy vampires even more, giving them that much more reason to single you out to kill.

The Wrists

The wrists might not have quite the blood flow of the carotid artery, but they're much easier to access. Emotional teenagers cut this same spot when nobody will notice them, an action usually done while listening to nu-metal (figure 27).

The Butt

The human butt has terrible blood flow, but it's just so degrading to the victim to be bitten there. It's the ultimate prank.

By biting somebody in the ass and letting that person turn into a vampire, that poor sucker will be forever known as the butt-vampire. Just like how being bitten in the butt by a pirate turns you into a butt-pirate.

Figure 27. "These wounds, they will not heal."

Hey, Now

This last area is a little iffy on whether you should use it or not. In both males and females, the reproductive organs have exceptional blood flow. The downside to this, of course, is accessibility.

In order to get to these areas, you pretty much have to get intimate with your soon-to-be victim. With a vampire's seduction skills, this shouldn't be too much of a problem, though. And don't worry about your vampire girlfriend thinking you're sleeping around. Remember, eatin' ain't cheatin'.

The Vampire Cookbook

The more culinary-inclined vampires often like to make special dishes out of blood.[53]

Black pudding, or blood pudding, is a type of sausage made by cooking blood with a filler (meat, bread, fat, barley, oatmeal, etc.) until it is thick enough to congeal when cooled. Blood soups and stews use blood as an ingredient in the broth. Other blood dishes include blood pancakes and fried blood. Doesn't that just sound delicious?

Mexico has a unique tradition of using tequila shots as well. To set it up, you first sprinkle some salt onto your hand. When you're ready, you lick the salt, take the shot, and then bite into your victim's neck. The salt makes the tequila go down easier and the alcohol acts as a disinfectant for whatever diseases are crawling around on your victim's skin.[54]

53. If only Martha Stewart would publish a blood-centric cookbook. Seriously, that woman is like a female MacGyver.
54. Seriously, Tijuana is pretty gross.

15. Let's All Go to the Movies

A discussion on vampirism wouldn't be complete without looking at the subject's influence in popular media. From comic books to video games to romanticized fantasy book series geared toward tweens,[55] vampires are a very popular subject.

The most prominent venue for vampires is undoubtedly in cinema, having played a large role in movies over the years, stretching as far back as black-and-white silent films such as 1913s *The Vampire*. Many of these movies have been incredibly influential, some because they were so entertaining or the portrayal of vampires was done so well, most others because they were so amazingly horrible. The following is a collection of both, preference to the latter.

---

55. Damn you, Stephenie Meyer.

Interview with the Vampire (1994)

Starring Brad Pitt as Louis de Pointe du Lac, Tom Cruise as the vampire Lestat de Lioncourt, and Kirsten Dunst as a little girl with probably just as elaborate a name, *Interview* revolves around Pitt's character and his devastatingly crushing depression. He is so unhappy that it gets to a point where he doesn't care if he lives or dies, and he's constantly pushing his luck all around town. I can totally empathize with his character; being rich and looking like Brad Pitt sounds like a horrible life. Cruise's character notices this and runs around trying to convert Pitt into an evil vampire. And a Scientologist.

Meanwhile, like in most of her roles, Kirsten Dunst does things while being all creepy and stuff.

Dracula (1931)

Hungarian-born Bela Lugosi play the lead role of Dracula in the first ever official Dracula film. Lugosi didn't speak any English, so for the film he was forced to learn his lines phonetically, resulting in amazingly eerie dialogue.

Long before he got the role, Lugosi claimed to have been attacked by a vampire, but with the whole "no English" thing who knows what the hell he actually said.

Jesus Christ Vampire Hunter (2001)

Jesus Christ has returned to Earth and he's here to kick some vampire ass. The city has plunged into a devastating shortage of lesbians and it seems that vampires are the cause of it. And only Jesus can save them. For the son of God, though, Jesus sure gets his ass kicked a lot. It almost puts *The Passion* to shame.

If hip, urban Jesus doesn't win you over, the atheist gang fights, a Mexican Lucha Libre wrestler named Santos, and a transvestite with a heart of gold sure will.

Blacula (1972)

In 1870, Prince Manuwalde, the ruler of an African nation, asks Dracula to help him suppress the slave trade. Dracula, of course, is a racist and instead turns the prince into a vampire and imprisons him in a coffin for almost two hundred years.

This awesome plot was successful enough to spawn several more blaxploitation-horror films such as *Blackenstein* and *Dr. Black, Mr. Hyde* as well as the pornographic spoof *Lust of Blackula*.

Nosferatu (1922)

A German expressionist, black-and-white, silent vampire film, *Nosferatu* is quite the genre bender. The film follows Count Orlok, which is really just a cheap appropriation of Count Dracula. In fact, the whole movie is an unofficial adaptation of Dracula. The filmmakers were unable to obtain the rights to the original novel, so instead, they just changed the names and some details and left it at that. This blatant moral disregard is easily the worst thing Germans have ever done.

Bordello of Blood (1996)

The majority of this film takes place in a whorehouse run by vampires, their headmistress played by Angie Everhart. Early in the movie, Corey Feldman visits the whorehouse to get some of that sweet vampire poontang. In order to prepare for this grueling role, Feldman personally visited over two hundred whorehouses all over the world. He's a very serious method actor.

Dennis Miller actually stars in the movie as a private detective, but really, who cares?

Blade (1998)

Wesley Snipes plays the titular character in this modernized vampire action movie. Aside from the usual weapons like stakes and a sword, Blade is also equipped with high-tech weaponry such as a bladed boomerang-like weapon, an aerosol can containing garlic extract and silver nitrate he calls "vampire mace," and a modified MAC-10 with silver-tipped, hollow-point bullets filled with liquefied garlic. Totally badass.

The original *Blade* was actually pretty good, but two progressively shittier sequels were made after its success. Snipes was a producer for the third film and got so pissed off that he launched a lawsuit against New Line because he was forced to give up screen time to his costars.

Now, his actions may seem a little absurd at first, but I'm

actually going to side with Snipes on this one. Jessica Biel is hot and all, but that's no reason to add a bunch of convoluted backstory about how she makes MP3 playlists on her iPod to listen to while she kills vampires. It's not even cool; it's just impractical.

Once Bitten (1985)

Jim Carrey plays a virgin who is discovered by a vampire who needs to drink a virgin's blood. So Jim Carrey gets laid. The End.

From Dusk Till Dawn (1996)

"Pussy, pussy, pussy! All pussy must go. At the Titty Twister we're slashing pussy in half! This is a pussy blow out! Make us an offer on our vast selection of pussy! We got white pussy, black pussy, Spanish pussy, yellow pussy, hot pussy, cold pussy, wet pussy, tight pussy, big pussy, bloody pussy, fat pussy, hairy pussy, smelly pussy, velvet pussy, silk pussy, Naugahyde pussy, snappin' pussy, horse pussy, dog pussy, mule pussy, fake pussy! If we don't have it, you don't want it! Take advantage of our penny pussy sale. Buy any piece of pussy at our regular price, you get another piece of pussy, of equal or lesser value, for a penny. Now try to beat pussy for a penny! If you can find cheaper pussy anywhere, fuck it! What's this? A new flavor approaching. Apple pie pussy."

Blood & Donuts (1995)

There's really only so much that can be said about this film. A vampire who has been recently awoken by getting hit with a golf ball falls in love with a woman who works at a donut shop. Yeah.

The IMDb page for this movie lists its plot keywords as "Nipples Visible Through Clothing," "Psychic Rape," and "Telekinetic Sex." Sounds like a winner if you ask me.

Buffy the Vampire Slayer (1992)

It's fairly common knowledge that the cult TV show was based on this movie, in which Kristy Swanson plays Buffy. It's also slightly less, but still fairly common knowledge that Keifer Sutherland's father, Donald, played Merrick, Buffy's original "watcher" in the film. But what not many people know is that the movie also features Ben Affleck. As "Basketball Player #10." Not only does he not get a name, but there were nine other dudes who were better at being nameless basketball player extras. He played the role beautifully.

Underworld (2003)

Underworld centers on Selene, a "death dealer," a vampire specially trained to hunt and kill werewolves, with whom the vampires have a long-lasting feud. Selene is played by Kate Beckinsale, making her officially the second hottest vampire of all time, right under Nosferatu. A sequel was made a few years later due to the popularity of the first film and an outcry from the public to see Kate Beckinsale in more tight leather. Not only were their prayers for leather answered, but they were also given one hot-ass, boner-inducing sex scene. Score!

Van Helsing (2004)

If *Alien vs. Predator* is any indicator, simply combining two similar franchises of popular movies does not result in box office gold. Hell, it doesn't even come close to getting bronze. So what happens when instead of two franchises you take seven or eight? You get one giant clusterfuck of a movie.

Van Helsing is the result of taking the Van Helsing character along with Dracula, Dr. Jekyll and Mr. Hyde, Transylvania, Igor, Frankenstein, werewolves, and an assload of little dragon vampire baby things and mashing it all up into a shitfest of CGI. Oh, and Van Helsing is supposedly the archangel Gabriel. A clusterfuck.

30 Days of Night (2007)

Alaska is an interesting place. It's cold, hardly populated, and once a year in the small town of Barrow, the sun doesn't rise for thirty days. Really, a lovely place to visit, especially if you're part of a group of vampires looking to kill everybody who lives there.

One would think thirty days is enough time to search a small town and kill all the residents, unless of course Josh

Hartnett lives there, in which case you'll wait to the very last day to force them out of hiding so Josh can heroically sacrifice himself to save the rest of the survivors. God, he's dreamy.

Embrace of the Vampire (1995)

Ever since the invention of cinematography, filmmakers worldwide have pondered the existence of a "Holy Grail" of cinema, a single aspect that would make any movie watchable, regardless of how insurmountably shitty it may be. In 1995, exactly one hundred years later, one such cinematic grail was discovered: Alyssa Milano's tits.

Embrace is a lot like the kind of movie you would expect to play late at night on Cinemax. It has an insignificant plot that serves no purpose but to fill the time between soft-core sex scenes. Don't get your hopes too high; this isn't real soft-core porn, but it's damn close. Alyssa gets naked and partakes in multiple sex scenes. Oh, and there might be a vampire or something, too.

The Lost Boys (1987)

The Lost Boys is a bit of a cult classic. It stars both Corey Feldman and Corey Haim, who (much) later went on to star in a horrible reality TV show called *The Two Coreys* that showed us neither had improved his acting skill since. The movie also stars Kiefer Sutherland as the leader of a small vampire gang. This was, of course, before he gained the ability to perform heroic terrorist-stopping feats in succinct one-hour blocks.

Twenty-one years later, a sequel was made, with Feldman reprising his original role. God help us all.

Princess of the Night (1990)

If the cover looks like a cheap porn movie, that's because it is. Some good, ol'-fashioned vampire porn. Lauren Hall stars as a vampire queen who particularly enjoys young male virgins. So, logically, there's a ton of oral. Other movies Hall has also starred in include *Breast Side Story*, *Deep Throat*, and *Cock Loving Moms*.

Vampire Chicks with Chainsaws (2006)

Here's a novel idea. Vampires can be incredibly scary, right? But what if they had chainsaws, too?! Has your mind been blown yet?

Vampires don't need chainsaws to kill people. Sure, chainsaws are intimidating, but if you're already a vampire I'm pretty sure that trumps the chainsaw's intimidation factor.

In addition to the unnecessary use of worn-out horror plot devices, the movie features various inconsistencies and errors. As YouTube user batcountryrox so eloquently points out: "ok hmmmmmm lets c vampires dont walk in day light."

John Carpenter's Vampires (1998)

John Carpenter, the master of horror, created a masterpiece of a vampire movie, doing what no other vampire movie director had ever done: cast James Woods in the lead role. Never before had a vampire hunter been portrayed so realistically: as a middle-aged man emotionally capable of only agitation and snarky sarcasm. He's the cinematic epitome of "mom's new boyfriend," the one who gets abusive when he drinks, except this time he's only a couple of beers in when he decides to go vampire hunting instead of beating you.

Dracula 2000 (2000)

While this attempt to transfer the story of Dracula over to a modern teen horror may have been a flop at the box office, the film offers a unique backstory to Dracula's origins: he was said to be Judas, one of Jesus's twelve apostles. Judas was the apostle said to have betrayed Jesus by handing him over to the Roman authorities. As punishment for betraying Jesus, he was denied admission into both Heaven and Hell, cursed to walk the earth for all eternity.

That's a pretty harsh punishment. Sure, he sent Jesus to be crucified and all, but it's not like he didn't come back a couple of days later.

Dracula.3000 (2004)

If the 3000 in the title doesn't make it obvious enough, the period in place of a space does: this movie is as futuristic as hell. The cover is a little misleading, though; there are no robot vampires in this movie. There are robots and there are vampires, but no robot vampires. It does have Coolio, though! That's gotta be a plus!

Like all good horror franchises, the writers took a popular archetype and (rather than using their creativity and imaginations) just did the same thing again, but in space!

The Little Vampire (2000)

Jonathan Lipnicki, the precocious little spiky-haired kid with glasses from *Stuart Little* and *Jerry Maguire*, stars as Tony Thompson, a lonely boy who just wants some friends. How adorable. He finds a new friend in the form of Rudolph, a vampire stuck in the body of a child.

Lipnicki spends most of the film saying stuff like "Dude!" and being adorably quirky, moistening the pants of six-year-old girls worldwide. Enjoy it, girls, before puberty has its way with him.

The Last Man on Earth (1964)

This is the classic apocalypse film that was remade twice, most recently as *I Am Legend*, starring Will Smith. Vincent Price plays Dr. Robert Morgan, a psychopath whose subconscious narrated every goddamn thing he did.

He'd obviously gone insane from being the last living man on the planet, but it's a bit disappointing they didn't put any attention on his unavoidable masturbation problem.

Revamped (2008)

Revamped is the cinematic equivalent of a car crash; it's a terrible thing to witness, but goddamn if it isn't entertaining. Movies that are so bad they're good aren't made on purpose. So on the rare chance one like this comes around, thank the omnipotent deity of your choice. Or just the guy who made the film; in this case, Jeff Rector.

Revamped was also written, directed, produced by and stars . . . Jeff Rector. Of course. The film even includes the (apparently) first ever vampire country western song, "Baby, You're a Pain in the Neck." Take a guess who wrote the song. Jeff Rector! That guy does everything! Poorly! He's like the white, untalented version of Tyler Perry.

Vampiyaz (2004)

You know a movie is straight flossin' when the title is purposely misspelled and uses *Z*s instead of *S*s. *Vampiyaz* revolves around a hip-hop ex-con who just got out of jail only to find his old neighborhood has been taken over by vampires. Homie don't play that.

The cover, which features the film's tagline, "Brothaz in blood," is actually pretty well done and professional looking, but don't let that fool you. The movie itself is utter shit and looks like it was filmed on a Handycam.

In one scene, a man gets robbed while he's asleep in a giant baby outfit. Top-shelf cinema, right there.

16. Other Media

In addition to appearing in cinema and in the imaginations of easily impressionable youth, vampire characters play prominent roles in several other areas of popular culture. Venues for vampirism stretch far and wide, including comic books like *X-Men: Apocalypse vs. Dracula* (2006), stage plays like *Dracula* (1924), and horrible musicals like *Dracula the Musical* (2004).

The role of vampires in popular culture is a varied one. At times, vampires are used as a pervasive metaphor for lust and the inherent destructiveness of humans' primal urges. Other times, they're a means of justifying all those sex scenes being added to your otherwise crappy horror movie. Whatever the reason, these creatures have become a staple of popular culture that won't be leaving anytime soon.

Buffy the Vampire Slayer (1997–2003)

As previously mentioned, *Buffy* was a hit TV show based on the 1992 movie by the same name. The character of Buffy was so interesting that Joss Whedon, the movie's creator and licensed occult historian, adapted the story once again as a TV series by the same name, starring Sarah Michelle Gellar.

The TV show became an instant cult hit, especially among creepy fanboys nationwide who supported the show through the creation of Buffy fan fiction (often focusing on Alyson Hannigan's character, Willow), running and maintaining Alyson Hannigan fan sites and Photoshopping Alyson Hannigan's head onto pictures of naked women.

Sesame Street (1969–present)

One of the famous vampires mentioned in chapter 1, Count von Count, plays a fairly prominent role in this longstanding children's morning television program. Sure, the Count is capable of teaching elementary math skills, but since when did it become a good idea to teach kids that vampires are friendly and can help you learn to count?

Do not let your children watch this show.

I'd rather my kids not know numbers than be misguided and susceptible to vampire attacks. That's just smart parenting.

"The Vampyre" (1819)

This short story written by John William Polidori follows a suave British nobleman—who is also a vampire—as he travels around London, Rome, and Greece killing pretty much everybody. The story is often attributed as the catalyst for the vampire romance genre.

See, before TV was invented, books were actually used as a form of entertainment. Nowadays, of course, they're just used to make you look intelligent while you try to pick up chicks at the bookstore or pass time while you poop.[56] In fact, there's a 73 percent chance you are doing one of those right now. And a 0.2 percent chance you're doing both simultaneously.

Sword of Dracula (2004)

Comic books have also had a significant influence in vampire literature. Oftentimes, vampires and vampire culture are used as metaphors. With *Sword of Dracula*, the world of vampires was modernized and used as an all-encompassing allegory for terrorism, with Dracula presented as "the Osama bin Laden of vampires."

The comic even featured Senator John Kerry in a Vietnam flashback where he led a Swift Boat in search of Dracula, something you'd never see a fictionalized version of George Bush ever doing. Even in made-up stories, he'd totally get his dad to help him skip out.

Vampire Hunter D (1983–present)

Vampire Hunter D is part of a series of Japanese novels that revolve around the titular main character, D, a half-human/

56. They're also great at balancing wobbly tables.

half-vampire lone wolf who hunts other vampires. The story takes place in the very distant future, around ten thousand years after a nuclear war has decimated the Earth. It's like a postapocalyptic version of *Blade*.

The story was later adapted into a manga series. For those uninitiated in the world of Asian-obsessed nerddom, manga are specifically styled comics and cartoons that while similar to normal comic books are somehow even nerdier. The kind of stuff that even other nerds would beat you up for.

Castlevania (1986)

It was only a matter of time before vampires found their way into the world of video games. In *Castlevania*, players fought against a wide array of monsters, including werewolves, Frankenstein, Medusa, the Grim Reaper, and, of course, Dracula himself.

The game was actually originally developed as a training simulator for prospective monster slayers, but it ended up being so fun and enjoyable to play that the developers marketed it as a video game for kids. It doubled as an entertaining video game and an antivampire youth-preparation tool!

You don't see good, educational games like that anymore. Nowadays, all they do is shoot innocent people and run over hookers. You don't need practice for that. Running over hookers is really, really easy. They even hang out on street corners, making them practically effortless to target.

BloodRayne (2002)

BloodRayne is a third-person, multiplatform video game that allows the player to control a half-vampire/half-human she-warrior who runs around killing Nazis. If that sounds badass it's because it totally is.

Like several games before it, it was later made into a horribly shitty movie, despite having a fairly impressive cast. The lead role of Rayne was played by Kristanna Loken, best known for her role in that horrible third *Terminator* movie as the female terminator. Am I blaming her for that movie sucking? Of course not. She was more than qualified to play an emotionless machine. She may not be the greatest actress in the world, but for her role in *BloodRayne*, all she really had to do was look hot and sneer every once in a while, two things she's quite capable of.

The supporting cast was much more impressive. Billy Zane! Udo Kier! Meat Loaf! They even had Ben Kingsley as the lead antagonist, for the love of God! They did, however, have to endure Michelle Rodriguez and her uncanny ability of always looking serious and angry.

And then of course there's Michael Madsen, whose performances seem to be entirely dependent on the director of his movies. Madsen in *Reservoir Dogs*? Incredible. Madsen in *Species II*? Eh, not so much. With *BloodRayne*, we're stuck with mediocrity, but really, we shouldn't expect too much with Uwe Boll at the helm.

If you're unfamiliar with Uwe Boll, he's the director responsible for making two other horrible movie adaptations of video games before *BloodRayne*: *House of the Dead* and *Alone in the Dark*. On IMDb and Rotten Tomatoes, two prominent movie websites highly regarded among critics and moviegoers alike, *House of the Dead* scored itself a 2.0/10 and 4 percent on the respective sites. *Alone in the Dark* netted 2.3 and 1 percent, respectively. With a track record like that, how can you *not* hire him?

For whatever reason, a sequel was made (with Boll behind the wheel once again) called *BloodRayne 2: Deliverance*, in which Rayne ventures into the Wild West of 1880s America to stop Billy the Kid,[57] who is a vampire, and his posse of vampire cowboys. If only this were a comedy . . .

The movie barely scored a 2.4 on IMDb and it didn't even rank on Rotten Tomatoes, although it does have four reviews listed (all negative of course). Perhaps the critics knew it was going to be bad and decided not to waste their time? Kristanna Loken seemed to think so before the movie was even made. She gave up her role to Natassia Malthe: equally attractive, equally unimpressive at acting.

You've really got to hand it to Boll, though. It's pretty impressive he was able to get the sequel made given how poorly

---

57. Perhaps it was Boll going outside the usual canon, but based on his accent, apparently Billy the Kid was originally from Russia or something. I'm guessing it was just horrid acting, though.

the original movie did. And on top of that, he was able to make one that was somehow even worse? That's a feat not many are capable of. They're even letting him do a third installment of the series slated for 2010 called *BloodRayne 3: Warhammer*. How does he do it?! He somehow managed to convince a movie studio to make another sequel to a franchise he's proven to be terrible with. In a genre that has consistently performed horribly. With a series that previously ended with the line, "Life is like a penis. When it's hard, you get screwed. When it's soft, you can't beat it." Jesus Christ.

The video game was actually pretty fun, though.

Twilight (2005)

The first in a series of novels by Stephenie Meyer, *Twilight* has spawned a veritable army of teenage girls who all want nothing more than to be romantically swept off their feet . . . by an emotionally challenged vampire.

It's billed in the vampire genre, but really, it's nothing more than a high school romance teen drama that just so happens to have a couple of vampires as characters. And they aren't even real vampires! There's zero concern of having their skin immediately burst into flame when hit with sunlight. Instead, it *sparkles!* They aren't afraid of dying; they're afraid of looking like they wear glitter. *Oh, the agony! The immortal torture!*

Fuck *Twilight*.

Blood Ties (2007)

Blood Ties is sort of like *CSI* with vampires. The show follows a cop–turned–private detective with a degenerative eye disorder[58] who's dating a 480-year-old vampire while she investigates supernatural crimes. It was not renewed for another season.

Also, it was on the Lifetime channel, so there was a ton of domestic abuse and dealing with emotions.

True Blood (2008–present)

Japanese scientists have created a synthetic blood substitute that stops vampires from being forced to feed on humans, allowing them to live in public among regular people. However, in a small Louisiana town, the normal townsfolk are still very much reluctant to let the vampires into society, a point illustrated by the sign in the opening credits that reads, GOD HATES FANGS.

Ugh.

Aside from a painful attempt at a vampire pun in the opening credits,[59] the show itself is an otherwise serious drama. Like any good vampire drama, the show features a generous use of metaphors, such as the town's vampires being looked upon as "outcasts" (metaphor for discrimination) and Sam's

---

58. Obscure illnesses add depth to characters!
59. A.k.a. the list of jackasses responsible for this abomination.

ability to shape-shift into a dog (metaphor for horrible plot devices).

Captain Britain and MI: 13 (2008–present)

Whereas *True Blood* simply alludes to the idea of racism through its metaphors for discrimination, Marvel Comics' *Captain Britain and MI: 13* tackles the topic head-on, focusing on Dracula's racial hatred of Muslims, which is, of course, based on historical information.

When Dracula was mortal, he fought against invading Ottoman hordes in Transylvania, possibly sparking this initial hatred. When Turkish representatives visited him in his throne room, they were asked to remove their turbans as per Romanian custom. They refused, stating it was against Muslim law to do so. He responded, "I will hammer in your law" and subsequently secured their turbans to their scalps by driving small iron nails into their skulls. "Bitches."

The comic touches on this when Dr. Doom, who is himself a racist, lectures Dracula about racism against Islam. You know your racism is getting out of hand when other racists think you're overdoing it.

Vampirella (1969–83)

Vampirella is a comic book series that ran for well over a decade, focusing on the fictional titular[60] heroine of

---

60. Hehhehehe, *tit*ular.

Vampirella—or Vampi, as she was sometimes referred to. It's always reassuring to have strong, female characters in lead roles. Young women need role models to show them the importance of being strong, the importance of being independent, the importance of wearing clothing that accentuates their cleavage beyond any reasonably justified means.

This lady ran around in basically stripper boots and one of the skimpiest bikinis imaginable. Of course, it's not very practical, but considering the comic's primary market was confined to the demographic of lonely, but perpetually horny nerds . . . it sold quite well.

The Historian (2005)

It's said that this book revolves around a modern-day retelling of the story of Dracula through the point of view of a historian in the 1970s. However, at 650+ pages, not a single person has been able to read the whole thing; thus, the true contents of this book remain a mystery.

Salem's Lot (1975)

This horror novel by Stephen King was his second to ever be published. Since then, two TV miniseries have been made based on it, the first in 1979 and the second in 2004. The cast of the 2004 version included, among others, Donald Sutherland, who played Buffy's "watcher" in the original Buffy movie. Dude sure likes vampires (in short bursts).

With most remakes, newer versions tend to follow the

originals fairly closely, updating only select details to modernize the story. The 2004 version did just that, following the 1979 version very closely . . . and adding cell phones.

> SOME DUDE
> Oh no! We are being chased by vampires!

> OTHER DUDE
> Do not worry, friend. I will use my...

> OTHER DUDE looks at the camera.

> OTHER DUDE (CONT'D)
> ...cellular telephone.

It was pretty half-assed.

Bunnicula (1979)

Bunnicula is a series of children's books featuring a vampire bunny that sucks the juice out of vegetables. So once again, we're confronted with children's entertainment involving vampires that doesn't even begin to mention how dangerous these creatures really are. Sure, we're supposed to be responsible and show kids the importance of eating their vegetables and all, but not when we do it without mentioning the dangers of vampirism. Shame on you, parents.

Hellsing (1997–2008)

This manga series chronicles the efforts of the Hellsing Organization (a.k.a. the Royal Order of Protestant Knights) in its fight against vampires and various supernatural foes in the United Kingdom. The series' main protagonist is Alucard, a vampire who works for the Hellsing Organization—the exact opposite of what a normal vampire would do. That's why his name is Dracula spelled backward, quite possibly the cleverest, most original plot device of all time. Now if you'll excuse me, I'm off to visit Nilbog to see my robot friend Tobor and look into the mirror of Erised. Redrum! REDRUM!

The Nymphos of Rocky Flats (2006)

Sometimes the plots to stories are boring, sometimes they're great, but every so often you come across a story so grand in proportion that everything else seems bland by comparison. This is one of those stories.

Nymphos, the first of a series of novels by Mario Acevedo, follows Felix Gomez, a soldier who has recently returned from fighting in Iraq and from the dead. Gomez is now a vampire, working as a private detective, investigating a string of murders used to cover up an outbreak of nymphomania at the U.S. Department of Energy's Nuclear Weapons Plant.

It's okay to feel blown away. It's understandable.

Other novels by Acevedo include *X-Rated Blood Suckers, The Undead Kama Sutra,* and *Jailbait Zombie,* all part of Acevedo's vampire PI series and not some sort of "horror porn," as one might assume.

The X-Files (1993–2002)

During this show's almost decade-long run, themes of vampirism were featured in a few select episodes. However, compared to some of the bizzaro crap they had on this show, vampirism was nothing special.[61] Hell, vampires are pretty tame compared to the discovery of a little alien fetus or a mutant serial killer harvesting people's kidneys to prolong his life.

Smallville (2001–present)

Smallville is a dramatic television series following the life of Clark Kent in his youth before he becomes Superman. Episode five of the fifth season featured a storyline involving vampires. The episode even featured James Marsters, who played Spike in *Buffy* and *Angel,* as a professor at Kansas University, where Clark Kent is a student. Oh, he can also make his fingers into long metal spikes àla *Terminator 2* to stab you in the chest. Worth noting.

In the episode, Lana Lang, after joining a sorority, is turned

---

61. "The truth, along with our writers' mental states, is out there."

into a vampire by the sorority sisters. Just goes to show how one woman's fear can be another man's fantasy.[62]

The vampires were the result of a piece of meteor rock infecting vampire bats that attacked a girl and turned her into the first vampire. That meteor is somehow the catalyst for everything on this damn show.

Apparently it just isn't enough to have a show about an alien with superpowers from another planet living with his adopted human parents and simultaneously dealing with the discovery of these powers and becoming an adult.[63] Sometimes, you have to insert vampires into your story to make it interesting.

---

62. A really weird, creepy man.
63. Super strength *and* puberty?! *Ack!*

A Brief Conclusion

When dealing with the world of vampires, the greatest skill you can have is not an ability to create makeshift stakes or crosses, but being able to think quickly on your feet.[64] A comprehensive knowledge of your enemy is your best chance at survival; however, the world of vampires is an ever-changing one. The information contained in these pages may be a start, but there is still much to be learned.

For example, research has shown that next to human blood, the only other "craving" vampires seem to have is for bite-sized, individually wrapped candy. For reasons still unknown, there seems to be a significant swell in candy-related vampire activity in late October of every year, almost as if they were taking part in an evil annual ritual or celebrating a holiday or something. During this time, hordes of vampires will go door-to-door, often with other unholy creatures in tow,[65] in search of these delicious treats.

Kill them immediately.

Even if they look like children, you must remember that

---

64. Although stakes really do help.
65. Like werewolves, witches, and overly protective parents.

these are bloodthirsty monsters who wouldn't hesitate to kill you first if given the opportunity. It's kill or be killed. Dispose of them as quickly as possible; you never know if another marauding group of these monsters is right next door.

If you aren't up for the slayer job you can attempt to bribe them with the candy they seek, but make sure you give them large helpings. And God forbid you give them fruit or spare change instead. Those who fail to provide a sufficient amount of candy are often met with a swift, but painful death. Or even worse, their front yard covered in toilet paper.

Other Horrific Consequences of Not Giving Out Enough Candy

- Perfectly good eggs ruined, thrown at house
- Doorbell rung, no one there when answered
- Bags of dog feces lit on fire on doorstep
- Decorative pumpkins smashed in driveway
- Car bomb

Along with the lack of information on vampires is a proportionally disturbing amount of misinformation. While this may hinder your search for the truth, hopefully this text has served as a strong starting point. It's up to you, the reader, to further understand and spread the truth. Like on Facebook or Twitter or something.

Dealing with vampires is a continual learning process.

Vampires are adaptive creatures; therefore, you must be as well. In this age of modern technology, advancements are coming left and right, especially in the form of communications. Adjusting with these emerging technologies is becoming more and more important with every passing day. As cool as it may sound to be a lonely hermit living in a trailer all alone, you really do need to keep yourself in the loop.

By using the Internet, for example, vampires are able to hunt for victims without even leaving their house, coaxing impressionable youth into meeting them at home like it's a vampire delivery service.[66] This new breed of online predators is killing off hundreds of dumb kids every month. Meanwhile, Chris Hansen has an entire team busy tricking sexual predators, and all they want to do is molest a few kids.

The key to avoiding vampire attacks is never letting your guard down and always being prepared. Stay aware. And remember, the most powerful item in your arsenal is not a stake or a clove of garlic, but a mock informative guide on vampires filled to the brim with fluff. Lots and lots of fluff. Tons of it, really. Nothing but sentence after incomplete sentence of useless words that serve no purpose but to make the page longer.

---

66. "Hey, you guys wanna order some Chinese?"

Fluff.

6/10